SpringerBriefs in Accounting

Series editors

Peter Schuster, Schmalkalden, Germany
Robert Luther, Bristol, UK

More information about this series at http://www.springer.com/series/11900

Peter Schuster

Transfer Prices and Management Accounting

Springer

Peter Schuster
Faculty of Business and Economics
University of Applied Sciences
Schmalkalden
Germany

ISSN 2196-7873 ISSN 2196-7881 (electronic)
SpringerBriefs in Accounting
ISBN 978-3-319-14749-9 ISBN 978-3-319-14750-5 (eBook)
DOI 10.1007/978-3-319-14750-5

Library of Congress Control Number: 2015931535

Springer Cham Heidelberg New York Dordrecht London

Printed on acid-free paper

Springer International Publishing AG Switzerland is part of Springer Science+Business Media (www.springer.com)

Preface

Transfer prices are of dominant importance in company practice and a decentralised organisation, e.g. a profit centre-organisation, is most widely used.

This textbook[1] takes an innovative controversial approach by looking at functions of transfer prices and how different types of transfer prices can fulfil them. It is partially the result of a planned book by the author originally, together with *Ralf Ewert* and *Alfred Wagenhofer*, building on their highly successful German textbook (2014) taking a wide approach and scope on Management Accounting, predominantly from a German perspective (their permission to use material derived from their German book is greatly appreciated).

Suggestions for transfer prices, commonly found in other textbooks, will be addressed and it will be shown why they do not contribute to solve the problems companies face. With the support of numerous examples and exercises a conceptual understanding of this most relevant management topic will be developed.

Transfer pricing is a part of most advanced courses on Management Accounting and/or Management Control and the analysis of transfer prices receives increasing attention. In almost all management accounting textbooks, it is usually covered in one chapter or perhaps only as a part thereof. This often leads to serious oversimplifications and reductions of contents. This book aims at filling this gap and to provide a concise and controversial view on the topic.

> Transfer prices are strongly linked to management control; therefore, their analysis from the management accounting and management control perspective is the focus of this book.

---

[1] This book's published version has benefited from helpful feedback, formatting support and suggestions by Mareike Hornung, Ruth Mattimoe and Robert Luther.

Learning Objectives

After studying this book, you should be able to:

- Understand the functions of transfer prices and cost allocations and the underlying conflict between coordination and profit allocation
- Analyse cost-based, market-based and negotiated transfer prices (in different forms) and their suitability (in general)
- Discuss market-based transfer prices in perfect and imperfect markets and the influence of synergies
- Understand marginal cost-based transfer prices for optimum coordination while being aware of the need to consider the problem of incentives and dysfunctional behaviour in the solution
- See the distortion of cost structures as a major argument against the use of full costs; apply an agency model based on full costs to show that the optimum transfer price is above marginal costs and that market prices would interfere with the solution
- Understand the applicability of multi-tier transfer prices for solutions possibly leading to optimum coordination
- See dual transfer prices as an optional choice for solutions possibly leading to optimum coordination and understand any difficulties and problems arising
- Discuss negotiated transfer prices as one type of transfer price
- Learn how to share risk under uncertainty and see the resulting behavioural effects
- Compare the ex-post and ex-ante views on transfer prices
- Show how to solve the capacity adjustment problem by the use of transfer prices and how to correct (i.e. punish) untruthful reporting by a specific transfer pricing mechanism
- Determine optimum transfer prices in a Nash equilibrium
- (In general:) Understand the effects resulting from asymmetric information and show potential misjudgements and incorrect decisions caused by transfer prices.

Contents

Chapter 1
Cost and Management Accounting

Abstract The accounting system deals with the conceptualisation and conditions of the company's information systems. The management accounting system supports the planning and coordination of company decisions and has two main functions: Decision-making (decision support) and behavioural control (decision influencing).

Keywords Accounting system · Management accounting · Cost accounting · Behavioural control · Decision support · Coordination · Management control

1.1 Content of the Accounting System

The accounting system deals with the **conceptualisation** and **conditions** of an organization's information systems. In principle, **management accounting** covers all information systems designed for the internal user, i.e. the manager as decision-maker in the company. In contrast, **external**—or **financial accounting**—is directed toward the external users, such as investors, creditors, customers, suppliers, competitors and the public.

The separation between internal and external accounting or management and financial accounting arises out of the different relationships between information **producer** and information **user** of the respective system. For **financial accounting**, the producer and the user are definitely different people; the producer essentially has a better state of information about the data that enter the system. Therefore, a high degree of regulation to guarantee a certain quality level of the information characterises this part of the accounting system. Legal rules support this, for example, for auditing and partly for specific agreements between producer and user (e.g. loan contracts). Often, the company as an institution is considered a monolithic block: as the producer of the information.

Management accounting can be understood in the sense that it fulfils its tasks free of legal and other restrictive rules. Conflicting aims and objectives with externals (for example stakeholders) do not seem to appear, at least at first glance.

P. Schuster, *Transfer Prices and Management Accounting*,
SpringerBriefs in Accounting, DOI 10.1007/978-3-319-14750-5_1

Yet, this does not imply that management accounting is free from conflicting objectives, they appear in the form of conflicts between decision-makers of different hierarchies within a company. The company's organisation and the resulting allocation of decision competences and responsibilities therefore gain essential importance for the management accounting system.

The **management accounting system** supports the **planning** and **coordination** of company decisions, particularly in the short run. The measures **costs** and **revenues** can be understood as the resource (goods) consumption, respectively production according to the company's objectives within a period. Usually they are derived from expenditures and yields.

1.2 Functions of Management Accounting

Management accounting has two **main functions**:

- **Decision-making** (decision support)—"influencing one's own decisions",
- **Behavioural control** (decision influencing)—"influencing other people's decisions".

According to the **decision-making function**, management accounting is an instrument of information as a basis for decisions made by management. **Conflicting objectives** are not considered further. Either there are no such conflicts if an individual acts (**one-person context**) or the company implicitly considers congruency of the objectives between the user, the upper manager and the producer of the information. This function can therefore be referred to as **influencing one's own decisions**.

Traditional management accounting literature mainly deals with this function. The concept and structure of accounting systems that deliver the best information supply support for **certain decision types**. **Information that is more exact** never impairs improvement of decision-making, as long as the **costs of information** are not considered. Only when the additional costs of information retrieval are fully considered and compared to gains caused by more precision it may become apparent whether the trade-off is favourable or not. Typical **decisions** that the management accounting system supports are related to the production schedule, the price determination or the procurement policy, as well as cost management. To be able to make suitable decisions, information about the cost amounts, the costs dynamics and possible effects are important.

1.3 Behavioural Control Function of Management Accounting

Decision support is at the centre of attention for the behavioural control function as well, but in a different way: it is to influence decisions made by others, i.e. **influencing other people's decisions**. This function explicitly considers the company organisation and is in the **multiple-persons context**. Decision-makers can have different targets on which they base their decisions.

Presuppositions for the behavioural control function are:

- There are—at least potentially—**conflicting objectives, aims or targets** between different decision-makers in the company. *Example*: a divisional manager strives for an increase in his staff[1] because the number of assistants assigned to him is an indication of his importance in the company.
- There is **asymmetrically distributed information** between the company's upper management and decentralised decision-makers. This is frequently the case: a divisional manager will have a better state of information about the details of his division than the head office will. After all, this is one main reason for the delegation of decisions to him.

The available information can be better utilised through delegation of decisions. However, company head offices also lose **possibilities for control**. *Example*: the company head offices often cannot assess the efficiency of the research department's activities because it possesses no specialised competence, or it can simply be a lack of time that prevents taking care and notice of all subordinate company divisions' activities.

There are a number of instruments to reduce conflicts of objectives and asymmetric information, such as delegation, monitoring or the appointment of suitable personnel. Management accounting can contribute to it as well, by the use of **management control information** and **coordination information**.

Management accounting enables the **cost** and **revenue control** of decision-makers. **Variance analysis** determines differences between budgeted and actually achieved values and a more exact analysis of their causes. This is meaningful not only for receiving knowledge of new environmental situations, but also for motivating the decision-maker to complete his tasks well since he is responsible for the variance. Control triggers a behavioural control effect in advance.

Management accounting also supplies decentralised decision-makers with information to be used for the **coordination** of decisions, and decentralised decisions can be subliminally influenced by it. *Examples*: if the management accounting information does not reflect the risk of decisions, a divisional manager may put inappropriate emphasis on it. If the costs of a central service (e.g. electronic data processing) are allocated based on the number of PCs in the departments, incentives arise to invest more in PC equipment, but not in the service activities of the service department. The coordination of the management system is an essential feature of the **management control** system, with instruments including budgeting, performance measures and—picked out in this book—**transfer prices** and **costs allocations**.

Transfer prices are strongly linked to management control; therefore, their analysis from the management control perspective is the focus of this book.

[1] The male gender used throughout the book is applied for matters of simplicity and without intention of any form of discrimination, nor to emphasise aspects of male versus female managers etc.

The **behavioural control function** can show peculiar effects on the organisation of the management accounting systems: the "correctness" and the precision suddenly may not be criteria anymore. More information is not always better, even without explicit consideration of information costs. With the **decision-making function** this was not the case: certainly management will not deliberately procure incorrect data for its own decisions. This does not always apply for influencing other people's decisions. A management accounting system that supplies more or less imprecise information that reduces information or delays reports can be advantageous. *Examples*: a divisional manager can use more information to better pursue his own aims and to make decisions, which are not optimal for the company as a whole. Too much information reduces the control options of the head office or the higher management. Aggregative information can induce the head office *not* to use individual performance measures; this can provide positive working incentives in the long term. On the sales side, upper management frequently demands full costs as a "lowest price-limit," despite knowing that the "correct" product costs for sales and price decisions are marginal costs. Many companies providing marginal product cost information to their sales representatives find that they are then too obliging in price negotiations.

This textbook emphasises management accounting's function of **behavioural control** as applied to transfer pricing in decentralised organisations. It is directed at the advanced reader. In the following section, the functions of transfer prices are considered first and then connected to the various types of transfer prices.

Chapter 2
Functions and Types of Transfer Prices

Abstract Transfer prices as the internal price of products created within the company have two main functions: profit allocation (in order to assess divisional profits and for performance measurement) and coordination (to come to decisions that are in the best interest of the company as a whole). Various types of transfer prices exist and are examined in view of these functions in the following chapters of this book: market-based, cost-based and negotiated transfer prices.

Keywords Management control · Decentralised organisation · Cost allocation · Profit centre · Synergies · Coordination · Asymmetrically distributed information · Conflicting objectives

2.1 Introduction

Transfer prices are values for inter-company products (intermediate products and services) that are purchased from (independent) company divisions, i.e. the **transfer price** is the internal price of products created within the company. One of the main functions of transfer prices is the coordination of the management of both the selling and the buying divisions. **Cost allocations** are a special form of transfer prices. They are transfer prices based on the cost of the producing company division and the sum of the allocated costs equal the costs incurred. Thus, if a higher amount is allocated to one division, another division will face lower amounts allocated.

The major presupposition for the need for transfer prices and cost allocations is a **decentralised organisation** with divisional managers **responsible** for performance measures of the division, typically the divisional profit or the divisional costs. Along with **budgeting systems** and **profit measures**, transfer prices are the most important instruments for **management control of divisional managers**.

Typically, divisions are organised as profit or investment centres within a company or legally independent subsidiaries. However, they can also be, for example, cost centres. In a profit centre, the divisional manager can decide about all

P. Schuster, *Transfer Prices and Management Accounting*,
SpringerBriefs in Accounting, DOI 10.1007/978-3-319-14750-5_2

operational business decisions and, therefore, is fully responsible for the profit of his division and is judged by it. Furthermore, it is supposed that divisional managers make their decisions to maximise their divisional profit. In the case of a cost centre, the revenues are assumed as being constant.

Production division are frequently organised as cost centres rather than profit centres. A **profit centre organisation**, however, can be meaningful when certain output characteristics are not directly measurable; an example is product quality (which often becomes obvious after sales). The profit centre organisation can induce important incentives (for example, by using the contribution margin of the sales division as the transfer price).

The idea of transfer price determinations is derived from the following considerations: transfer prices are based on the fiction of a "**market**" within the company. The divisions are supposed to act like independent companies, and this has the advantage that the decision delegation to subordinated employees and managers should lead to entrepreneurial conduct. The ability to coordinate is expected by the internal (fictitious) market; however, the external market is expelled by the internal organisation of the company. Therefore, the integration of all divisions within one single company must lead to advantages compared to independent companies, because the integration also causes costs. Apart from missing the adjusting effect of the external market, costs of the coordination (including those caused by the use of transfer prices) appear. Without coordination, the advantages of integration would hardly work, and then independent companies would be better. Empirical studies confirm this. It is to be noted, of course, that integration for tax reasons can certainly count (an example is the enabling of an immediate loss of compensation if such was not possible with legal independence). **Advantages of integration** lie, for example, in improved capacity utilisation, the decrease of quality tests, in lower marketing costs by utilisation of the company reputation or by improved access to identical market segments, in better coordination of product developments as well as the use and concealment of knowledge and expertise. Such advantages generally come from a lowering of the transaction costs. These are less technical circumstances than the better use of information or the improvement of the bargaining position. These effects appear when and because markets are not perfect. Now, decentralisation and transfer prices again bring the market into the company. The problem is finding a transfer price that combines as many advantages as possible in relation to its disadvantages. It is obvious that transfer prices must always be seen in **connection** with the **company's organisation**.

2.2 Functions of Transfer Prices

The most essential functions of transfer prices (for internal use) are:

1. **Profit allocation** in order to assess divisional profits and for performance measurement,
2. **Coordination, influence and guidance** of the divisions,

3. **Calculation and cost accounting** for decisions and for price justification,
4. **External regulatory purposes**, especially for balance sheet and income statements and
5. **Simplification** (transfer price is applied as normalised budget measure).

Profit Allocation
In decentralised companies, transfer prices are necessary for the determination of the divisions' profits, when there are linked performances between the divisions. On the one hand, the transfer price is the (internal) revenue of the supplying division; on the other hand, it indicates the (internal) purchase cost of the buying division. **Divisional profit** is the basis for decisions of both divisional management and the company's upper management, which uses it for strategic activities or budget allocations. It also serves for the assessment of divisional management's performance. The profit contribution of every division thereby becomes visible, the responsibilities are clearly presented, and cost transparency and cost awareness are promoted.

The determination of divisional success requires an accurate demarcation of the success components, which can be assigned to the different divisions. When performance is to be measured divisional profits have to be allocated, thus profit allocation is an important function of transfer prices.

Yet, the demarcation is difficult for example, when two or more divisions are interwoven with each other. The **interweaving** can appear in the following cases:

- Products of one division are bought in by another division (**sequential interweaving**). *Example*: a division produces an intermediate product, which is processed further by another division, made into a final product and sold at the market.
- Divisions compete for limited resources (**resource interdependencies**) or on a common (limited) sales market (**market interdependencies**); it is a joint resources group. *Examples*: two divisions produce substitute products, or two divisions need a quality test for certain components during their production processes, which is executed by a special department that is at its capacity limit.

The success that appears as a result of common products is also named **synergistic effect**. It cannot be split or divided on the basis of the individual divisions' contributions. From a theoretical view, it is impossible to execute such a correct split-up, as the success results by common products only. Should one division be eliminated, the synergetic effect would be appropriately shortened or completely ceased. It might be possible to determine limits and ranges of such losses as a result of a division's erasure, or it might be possible to apply an average principle or to split up the effects equally. However, all these possibilities are arbitrary.

> **Quote**
> Trying to defend an [...] allocation is like clapping one's hands, then trying to defend how much of the sound is attributable to each hand. (Ijiri 1967, p. 13).

Shapley value
The Shapley value tries to create a "fair" split-up of synergistic effects based on a concept of the cooperative game theory. For this, all possible coalitions of the contributing divisions are considered, and it is asked which advantage appeared, if now the considered division is included. Then the Shapley value arises as a weighted average value of the marginal advantages with every given coalition. Although this can be seen as a "fair" result, the Shapley value also remains arbitrary, just like any other split-up.

Example Division B1 of a company constructed a brand name by intensive marketing activities at a cost of 1,000. The brand name has received a very positive image among consumers. B1 achieves a contribution margin of 10,000. Now, another division, B2, would like to use this brand name for one of its products. B2's contribution margin rises with the brand name's use by 1,000–5,000. How high are the divisional profits of B1 and B2? The use of a brand name constructed within the company is a synergistic effect. If division B2 had to construct its own brand name, this would be relatively expensive and probably less effective than the use of the already established name.

Coordination Function
Divisional managers should work hard and make their best efforts in their division. Incentives are given to maximise their divisional profit. This can guide them to make decisions that are favourable and profitable from the perspective of their own division, but unfavourable from the view of the company as a whole. The effects of a division's decisions on other divisions are **externalities** that are not considered by their divisional manager.

Examples

1. The marketing department promised a customer an extremely short delivery time, and to achieve this, the production department must deviate from their optimised production programme or must delay maintenance works.
2. The optimal market treatment from the perspective of Division 1 is to start a price war with a competitor, but it contradicts the company's strategy of following a high price strategy for all products.
3. A production division could achieve cost savings (producing a positive net present value) through an investment in the automation of the manufacturing process. However, it is forced to pass on part of the cost savings to the buying divisions by which the net present value of the cash flows from the perspective of the division will become negative. Therefore, it refrains from the investment.

The transfer prices can now be used to **influence** decentralised decisions. Assume that the divisional manager is responsible for short-term decisions. The head office announces a transfer price (or a transfer price scheme) to the manager for inter-company transfer of intermediate products. The decision behaviour of the manager can be steered by influencing the divisional profit through the transfer price. A higher transfer price in tendency reduces the amounts bought-in by the purchasing division, to choose another production procedure, or to accept a one-off special order less easily. A higher transfer price can change the producing division's production programme or the production amounts. Examples of such behavioural control effects will be given later in this chapter.

Coordination function is the term used throughout this book. A similar concept is sometimes described as "goal congruence" and suboptimal decision as "incongruent decisions". We prefer the abstract term of "coordination (function)" as the goals of different divisions usually will not be 100 % identical and the perspective on goals only seems too limited. Coordination, in contrast, indicates the main function and stresses the linkage to behaviour guidance and **management control**, for example of the divisional managers' decisions by the head office of a company.

Other Functions

Transfer prices fulfil a number of other functions besides profit allocation and coordination, for example **calculation** for the determination of factors used in central decision-making when several divisions are involved or in affiliated group companies. The cost accounting system of such companies traces the relevant costs between different, legally independent divisions, used for price calculations. The determination of **costs of goods produced** for external regulatory purposes or rectifications of prices against third parties are other functions of transfer prices.

From a company perspective, a predominant issue is the optimisation of **taxes** and related payments. Transfer prices of multi-national corporations are often influenced by such considerations. These effects are ignored in this book, as profit allocation in that sense equals the manipulation and the allocation of profits to regions and countries that minimise tax payments for the company. As the title, "Transfer Prices and Management Accounting", suggests this book takes the approach of management accounting, i.e. the **managerial use of accounting information for decision-making** respectively with emphasis on the **decision-influencing** aspect. The OECD publishes guidelines for transfer prices in order to limit manipulation and applies the so-called arm's length principle. We ignore this perspective and relate our line of argumentation to the **management accounting view** and its **direct relationship to decisions**, in the described way, i.e. we focus on **coordination** and **profit allocation** in the described sense.

Empirical results

The "*Transfer Pricing 2003 Global Survey*" by *Ernst and Young* (2003) questioned 641 financial managers of internationally active parent companies and 200 managers of subsidiaries from 22 countries about their transfer pricing policies, with tax versus management targets playing an important role. 80 % of the group companies preferred uniform transfer prices for both tax related and management related decisions. 40 % of the parent companies responded that management aspects were more important than fiscal issues, and for 25 % of the mother companies, the support of the company strategy were the exclusive driver of the transfer price policy.

In a similar study by *Deloitte* (2006), there were 240 companies with consolidated annual sales in excess of €500 million located in Germany. The four most important objectives of a transfer price system were shown as internal profit allocation, the support of the group strategy, the optimisation of company taxation and the control system for resource allocation. The companies confessed that not all objectives could be pursued simultaneously, and the top performer focused on the internal control (and, therefore, less on fiscal) aspects than the other companies.

In a questionnaire of Swiss companies, Pfaff and Stefani (2006) found that the majority of companies used uniform transfer prices for both external and internal functions. Market and full cost-based systems were predominant, and the companies seemed to classify the importance of synergistic effects for internal control as less important.

Transfer prices between legally independent company divisions are of special importance. In **commercial law** transfer prices are important when the participation ratios of mother company and daughter company are not identical (for example, if the daughter company has minority shareholders); then the **profit allocation function** is the focus of attention: the achieved profit should be divided "fairly" and "righteously" between the divisions to avoid discriminating against the minority partner. Effects caused by **tax law** can be seen similarly, as the total amount of taxes due can largely depend on the profit allocation, most obvious with transnational sales. The OECD has legislated directives for internationally uniform transfer price methods that are recommended. A "correct" division of the profit earned in connection with several divisions, nevertheless cannot succeed unambiguously and without doubts, and therefore companies have a certain leeway.

Finally, another function of transfer prices is the **simplification** of the cost accounting system by use of **normalised measures**, frequently only to keep exogenous fluctuations of the input prices out of analysis.

Asymmetrically Distributed Information

Typically, models for the determination of transfer prices implicitly assume symmetrically distributed information: the head office has all the necessary information about the divisions, and with it could solve the coordination problem itself. At the same time, a need for the profit allocation function would not exist either, as the head office possesses all information anyway. Exaggerated, it could be said that transfer prices solve a problem that does not exist at all.

In a more realistic view, information will be **distributed asymmetrically**: the respective divisional manager is better informed about his division than the head office. Several examples are shown throughout this book about **misleading control** effects that can be caused by certain transfer prices because of better information of the divisions.

Asymmetrically distributed information not only has the effect that the head office can make less precise decisions, but also leads to the fact that divisional managers cannot be **assessed** by their real performance, but rather based on surrogates only. Such a surrogate is the **divisional profit**, which was already used in the previous discussion. With it, the objective of the divisional manager differs from the objectives of the company as a whole (i.e. conflicts of interest arises).

Conflicting Objectives

The different functions of transfer prices frequently are **competitive** to each other. A transfer price that fulfils one function very well can be unsuitable or even counterproductive for another function. Particularly, the conflict of objectives between the two functions **profit allocation** and **coordination** is vast. *Example*: the company likes to provide considerable leeway for price setting to the division that sells externally at the market. For this, it is seen as necessary that marginal costs are applied to intermediate products sold within the company, because in the short-term perspective they equal the only relevant cost. With linear cost functions, the selling divisions producing these intermediate products, end up with a loss in the amount of their total fixed costs potentially resulting in a high divisional loss, while the purchasing division gains the total contribution margin. For the function of profit allocation, such divisional profits are worthless and meaningless. It applies similarly to other functions, such as the tax-optimal determination of transfer prices. Such transfer prices are often very unfavourable for management control issues.

Conflicts of objectives are frequently found within the same function. Assume that the head office would like to limit the demand for an internally produced product. One possibility is setting a high transfer price for it, as the purchasing division would reduce demand if possible. At the same time, the head office needs undistorted measures for their own decisions, for example, the allocation of resources to the divisions, and a transfer price set too "high" is unsuitable for this.

Such conflicts of objectives can be solved in a relatively simple way, by the use of **different transfer prices**, one for every function. Every division determines two or several divisional profits, for example, one used for the manager's assessment and another indicating the "real" profit. However, this solution frequently meets with difficulties in the reality of company practice. How could it be explained that a divisional manager must pay marginal costs of the internal product (for coordination purposes), while his divisional profit is determined based on higher costs, with the profit used for measuring and assessing his performance? The coordination takes place just by the fact that the performance measure (divisional profit) is manipulated in a way that divisional managers autonomously make decisions in the best interests of the company as a whole. In other words: "*In some cases, the impression is given to the divisional manager that he is playing a bookkeeping game*" (Dearden 1962, quoted by Thomas 1980, p. 209). However, if the assessment is disconnected from this manipulated profit, the coordination function of the transfer price could not be reached at all.

Another problem arises: typically, the **divisional profit** is dependent upon **strategic decisions** made by the head office. The divisional manager can raise his profit if he receives higher resources. With this mechanism, the "real profit", following the function of profit allocation, will create reactions in the co-ordination and control system. For example, the manager will align his decisions not only with the transfer price installed as part of the management control system, but also with maximising the "other" profit that will raise his profit through resource allocation. As a result, the head office cannot receive an undistorted divisional profit and must also consider these incentives. With it, the profit allocation function is absorbed to a certain extent by the management control function.

For these reasons, companies usually use only one transfer price, and it arises from balancing the effects of different transfer prices on the respective functions.

Other optional solutions of the conflicts of objectives are interventions in the decision autonomy of the divisions, for example, obligations of delivery and purchase commitments or restrictions, or changes of the organisational structure or the incentive system. Other performance measures, such as productivity ratios, could replace divisional profit. Profit as a criterion has enough disadvantages by itself: profit is typically short-term based and highly aggregated. At first glance, a renunciation of the determination of separate divisional profits and the divisional managers' assessment based on the joint profit (profit sharing) appears to be a way out of the dilemma; however, there are also a number of negative side effects. Since every divisional manager is only connected to a small part of the positive and negative success, he can prefer to reduce his individual efforts and to use them otherwise. How could motivation of decentralised decision-makers be achieved if they depend on profit figures that can only be found centrally, more or less in one account for all divisions?

2.3 Types of Transfer Prices

In theory and in practice, a multiplicity of transfer price types is used. They can be summarised and categorised into three major **types**:

- **Market-based** transfer prices,
- **Cost-based** transfer prices,
- **Negotiated** transfer prices.

All three types are often used in practice and the most frequently used type is the cost-based transfer price, followed by the market-based transfer price.

The significance and informative value of such examinations suffer from the fact that the three types of transfer prices are **not entirely free of overlap**. *Example*: A construction and engineering company applies costs as a basis for its market prices (i.e. offers) and negotiates these prices in the following way. For internally produced intermediate products that show the same characteristics it is unclear as to whether the transfer price is market-based, cost-based or negotiated. Often, companies use several types of transfer prices simultaneously.

The operations research literature also explored transfer prices from different perspectives (the interested readers of this book will find some references at the end of this book).

2.4 Organisational Settings

For the **practical application** of transfer prices, criteria like **simplicity** and **acceptability** play an important role in practice. What use does a very ingeniously devised transfer price system have if no user is able to understand and administrate it? For acceptability, it is essential to know whether the transfer prices lead to divisional results that are considered fair.

Therefore, apart from the choice of the type, the following **questions** need also to be answered:

- Who determines the transfer price?
- What duration does the transfer price have, and what are the circumstances when it must be decided upon anew?
- Is the transfer price chosen permanently or dependent upon production volume?

Often transfer prices are only set for key products, while all other products transferred in insignificant amounts are based on simple rules such as market prices applied.

Transfer prices cannot be assessed without consideration of the **company's organisation**. Of particular importance for the function of transfer prices is the decision scope that the divisional manager possesses. In companies certain organisational conditions, so-called **rules**, are defined for this. Among other things they are:

- Does one or every division have the choice to partially or fully buy in from the market, or is there a strict rule to buy/sell internally?
- Are there priority rules for internal sales?
- Can a division freely make an external agreement at its conditions (last call)?
- To what extent must central services be bought internally?
- May a division produce a product themselves even if another division produces the same product?
- Up to which volume can a divisional manager make investment decisions?
- Can a divisional manager select staff?
- What are the informational obligations and ways between divisions?

Remark
It is more difficult to work inside than externally. In the smallest impasse, a person can go up the line. Nobody wants to have the boss coming and making accusations of not cooperating. It is always difficult, so you need a financial incentive or something else, such as recognition for being a good corporate citizen (An anonymous manager quoted in Kaplan and Atkinson 1998, p. 455).

This chapter first discusses **sequential production** in vertically integrated companies. In their most simple form, there are only two divisions, a producing and a purchasing division. It becomes more difficult in cases where the producing division also manufactures other products (how are the indirect costs allocated?), and cases in which several divisions buy the internal products. **Resources and market interdependencies** are discussed afterwards; it mainly focuses on **competition** among the "purchasing" divisions for the limited resources of the producing division. The resource consumption is to be controlled, often by the head office or a service centre.

Chapter 3
Market-Based Transfer Prices

Abstract The market-based transfer price seems to be the natural option to support the idea of decentralised decision-making and is favoured by many text-books. This books uses examples in perfect and imperfect market settings and explains reasons why other types of transfer prices are more likely to fulfill the desired functions, i.e. reliable profit allocations and figures on the one hand, and decisions in the best interest of the company as a whole on the other.

Keywords Market-based transfer price · Dealing at arm's length rule · Synergetic effects · Perfect market · Imperfect market · Modified market price

3.1 Applicability of the Market Price as Transfer Price

The choice of the market price of a product that is equivalent and comparable to the intermediate product is one option for the determination of a transfer price. Ideally, the following **conditions** must apply:

1. A market for the intermediate product or a full substitute exists. In reality this condition is often not fulfilled, as several products with different prices are offered, which can serve more or less well as a substitute for the internal product.
2. Transactions of the company divisions may have no influence on the market price, as otherwise, the divisions could affect the price. Nevertheless, this condition is fulfilled when perfect competition exists.
3. There is a uniform market price. If the market price is affected by the order amount or if a certain order sum changes within a period (for example, by discounts), which price should then be taken?
4. The market price should fit the decision. It should not be affected by short-term price considerations (for example, cut-price offers). For that reason, "finding" a price by an external offer might be problematic because the offer may be very low, simply set to clinch a business relationship with the expectation of later being able to raise the price when in a constant business relationship.

P. Schuster, *Transfer Prices and Management Accounting*,
SpringerBriefs in Accounting, DOI 10.1007/978-3-319-14750-5_3

The better these conditions are fulfilled and the more efficient the market for an intermediate product, the more suitable is the market price as the transfer price. Then, such a transfer price is suitable to be applied for the divisions' **profit allocation** as every division simply can have a comparison with the market situation. It is also suitable for **coordination**. A coordination requirement mainly appears as a result of synergistic effects, but these synergies do not exist in perfect markets, and thus coordination is virtually guaranteed by the market. However, in practice such markets or market prices are more the exception than the rule. Markets are typically imperfect—this is a reason why companies exist and are economically meaningful, as already shown. Therefore, in this case approximate solutions must be used.

Remark

The recommendation of *Anthony*, *Dearden* and *Govindarajan* (1992, p. 233 f.) for the transfer price is: "*If the market price exists (or can be approximated [...]), use it.*"

Another advantage of a market price that fulfils the above conditions is the **low manipulability**, as the market price does not depend on the (better) state of information of divisional managers and to a certain extent, is rather an "objective" measure. With legal repercussions and effects, for example, if the divisions are legally independent, the market-based transfer price is recognised as being probably the best solution of the profit split-up between the divisions.

From a taxation point of view, the **price comparison method** corresponds to this transfer price type and is based on the so-called **dealing at arm's length** rule requiring an external reference price, with a price offered to a third party (inner price comparison), and a price coming up between exclusively third external parties (external price comparison). Comparable conditions are required, such as the product qualities, additional components, risk taking, the conditions and the economic situation. Another approach is to use the resale price, applied especially between mother companies supplying to daughter distribution companies; the transfer price arises on the basis of the retail price reduced by the usual market profit margin.

From a long-term view, **market prices** have an indicative function about the profitability of company divisions. If a division in the long-term view and at future market prices cannot earn profit (not: contribution margins), the company probably would be better off without this division, and selling it should be considered (investment appraisal methods need to be applied for the decision-making).

In summary, market-based transfer prices will tend towards being more appropriate and suitable:

- The more efficient the market,
- The smaller the **synergistic effects** and
- The smaller the volume of the internal sales.

In the described cases, the potential disadvantages hardly impair the advantages of market prices. However, it is obvious that under these conditions, little needs to be coordinated.

If the divisions can access the **external market unrestrictedly**, the transfer price (in the following called R) must equal the **market price** for the intermediate product or the internal service p_I, as otherwise no internal transfer would occur. The reason: first, $R \geq p_I$ must apply; as otherwise, the producing division would only deliver to external buyers. At the same time $R \leq p_I$ applies as otherwise the purchasing division would not buy anything internally and would use the external market. Therefore, $R = p_I$ arises.

The use of market prices is not limited to situations when the divisions may actually use the market for intermediate products. Upper management can impose the policy that existing internal demand or supply has to be acknowledged. Vice versa, company policy may leave the decision about the extent of the inter-company business at the discretion of the divisions. This should bring "competition" into the company. With a view on price decisions, however, this can be problematic. Dependent upon the price calculation as well as the economic situation of competitors, incorrect decisions from the view of the company as a whole can arise.

Example

Division 1 produces an intermediate product, which is processed further into a final product by Division 2 and then offered at the market. This example relies on the simplifying assumption that the final product requires exactly one unit of the intermediate product (the consumption coefficient equals one). This is not restrictive, as with other consumption coefficients the amounts of the intermediate product or that of the final product only need to be adapted. The market price for the final product amounts to $p = 200$. The intermediate product is sold at a market price of $p_I = 120$ without limits. In Division 1 the variable production costs are $c_I = 90$, the costs of processing and sales in Division 2 amount to $c_2 = 20$ (Case 1) or alternatively $c_2 = 40$ (Case 2). Division 2 now receives an inquiry for a supplementary order at a price of $p = 150$ per unit. The acceptance of this additional order has no effect on the regular sales volume. In order to show the problems, it is assumed that both divisions have sufficient free capacities. Figure 3.1 shows

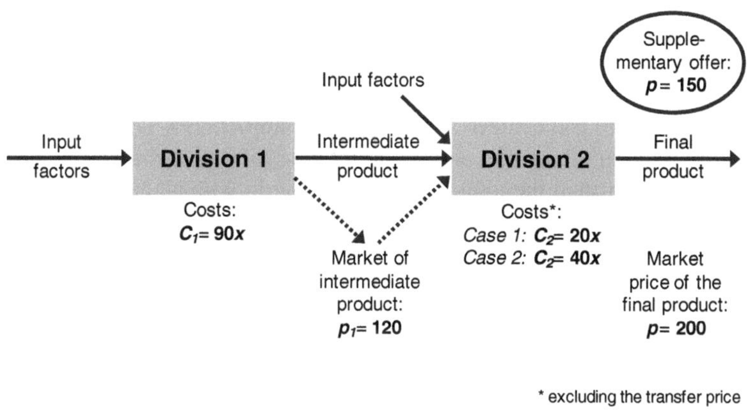

Fig. 3.1 Perfect market for the intermediate product

Table 3.1 Contribution margins in a perfect market

Division 1		
Transfer price		120
Variable cost		−90
Contribution margin of the supplementary order		+30
Division 2	Case 1	Case 2
Sales price	150	150
Variable cost	−20	−40
Transfer price	−120	−120
Contribution margin of the supplementary order	+10	−10
Company	Case 1	Case 2
Sales price	150	150
Variable cost of Division 1	−90	−90
Variable cost of Division 2	−20	−40
Contribution margin of the supplementary order	+40	+20

this situation. Should Division 2 accept the order, and should Division 1 supply the intermediate product?

The perspective of the divisions and the company as a whole are summarised in Table 3.1.

The use of the market price as the transfer price for the intermediate product causes both divisions to be **indifferent** as to whether they supply inside, sell or buy in externally. Division 2, for example, might as well buy the intermediate product at the market.

In Case 1, both divisions determine a positive contribution margin if the supplementary order is accepted. Therefore, both choose this option. The total contribution margin achieved equals the sum of the two divisions' contribution margins ($30 + 10 = 40$).

In Case 2, Division 2 determines a negative contribution margin and, therefore, rejects the supplementary order. At first glance, this hardly appears profitable from the company's perspective. Yet, it is the optimal decision, as Division 1 now can sell the intermediate product required for the rejected supplementary order at the market for $p_I = 120$ and achieve a contribution margin of 30. This equals the total contribution margin attainable, as Division 2 can gain no additional contribution margin. It is higher than the total contribution margin with an amount of 20 when the supplementary order was to be fulfilled. Thus, the acceptance of the supplementary order is not optimal from the total company perspective, too. Again, the market price entirely fulfils the coordination function. The market for the intermediate product is perfect.

This example requires the existence of sufficient **free capacities** for the supplementary order. The other assumption in the example, namely the constant market price without sales limits and constant variable cost leads to the fact that the full capacity utilisation is optimal in both divisions' perspective. Therefore, the assumption of free capacities implicitly requires further assumptions; for example, the existence of long-term relationships concerned with the delivery, could explain this.

When the **capacities** were fully **exhausted**, the following solution would arise: for an acceptance of the supplementary order, Division 1 would have to redirect the required units of the intermediate product from the market sales to Division 2. Then the additional contribution margin of the supplementary order would equal zero, and Division 2 would always reject this order because it prefers the market price $p = 200$ against the price of the supplementary order of $p = 150$.

Supply and sales limitations cannot lead to improvements but act to reduce profits instead. Limitations have an effect only if the transfer price is determined at a price not identical to the market price. *Example*: assume $R = 100$. Then Division 2 would accept the supplementary order and determine a divisional contribution margin of $150 - 40 - 100 = 10$, and Division 1 would supply (although reluctantly) because its divisional contribution margin amounts to $100 - 90 = 10$. However, this decision is not optimal from the perspective of the company as a whole because it prevents Division 1 earning a divisional contribution margin of 30 at the external market.

Assume that Division 1 cannot sell any additional amounts of this intermediate product at the market. Then the favourable choice (also from the company view) is lost, and the acceptance of the supplementary order becomes the optimal solution. However, Division 2 will still not be willing if the transfer price remains at the market price. The transfer price might not exceed 110 ($=150 - 40$), and it could even be lowered down to 90 ($= c_I$), at which price Division 1 is still ready to supply the intermediate product.

Extension of the example

Division 1 has variable production costs of only 90 in the case of internal delivery; for external sales, additional variable costs of 16 appear as a result of additional sales activities, leading to increased variable costs of $90 + 16 = 106$. The variable costs of processing and sales are 40 in Division 2 if the intermediate product is purchased internally and are 50 if bought in from the external market due to additional quality tests and freight charges. Figure 3.2 shows the modified situation.

Again, the perspective of the divisions and the company as a whole are summarised in Table 3.2.

Applying a transfer price equal to the market price, Division 2 again determines a contribution margin of the supplementary order in the amount of -10 and, therefore, rejects the order. If Division 2 buys in externally, the negative contribution margin gets even worse due to additional costs of 10 and becomes -20. Division 1 can sell the respective amounts of the intermediate product not required by Division 2 at the market and achieves a positive contribution margin of $120 - 106 = +14$ per unit. Based on a transfer price equal to the market price, this is also the total contribution margin in decentralised decision-making.

However, it is lower by 6 than the contribution margin of 20 that would arise for the company as a whole, with the acceptance of the supplementary order. Consequently, with existence of synergies, the market price no longer leads to the

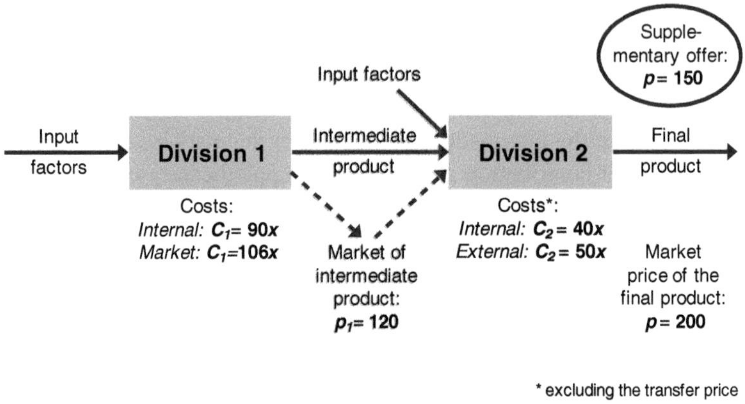

Fig. 3.2 Imperfect market for the intermediate product

Table 3.2 Contribution margins in an imperfect market

Division 1		
Sales	Internal	External
Transfer price	120	120
Variable cost	−90	−106
Contribution margin of the supplementary order	+30	+14
Division 2		
Purchase	Internal	External
Sales price	150	150
Variable cost	−40	−50
Transfer price	−120	−120
Contribution margin of the supplementary order	−10	−20
Company		
Division 1's sales	Internal	External
Sales price	150	120
Division 1's variable cost	−90	−106
Division 2's variable cost	−40	–
Contribution margin of the supplementary order	+20	+14

optimal coordination, as Division 2 makes a decision that is suboptimal, i.e. incorrect, from the perspective of the company as a whole.

Does a transfer price exist in this situation leading to the optimal decision? Such a transfer price must guarantee a positive (additional) contribution margin for both divisions against the best alternative in each case (opportunity costs). Division 1 supplies to Division 2 at every price higher than its variable cost (including opportunity costs), so the internal sales are 90 + 14 = +104. Division 2 accepts the supplementary order at every transfer price lower than 110. Every transfer price within the following interval: $104 \leq R \leq 110$ leads to the optimal decision from the company's perspective, i.e. fulfils the coordination function. At what exact price within the given range the transfer price should be set, at first depends on whether it is given by the head office or is negotiated. A fair possibility is the equal subdivision of the additional contribution margin of 6, which leads to a transfer price $R = 107$. The results of these examples show a **general understanding**:

A transfer price leading to decentralised decisions that are optimal decisions from the perspective of the company as a whole, often does not correspond to the market price of the intermediate product. Market-based transfer prices do not fulfil the **coordination function**.

The market price is only relevant through the amount of the opportunity costs (in the example: external sales with a contribution margin of $120 - 16 - 90 = 14$) and so far plays a role in the decision. It determines the lower limit of the possible transfer price.

3.2 Modified Market Price

It is by no means compelling to exactly use the market price as a transfer price. Actually, company practice sees different forms of modifications of the market price. One frequently used is the following modification:

Market price of intermediate product sold internally
− Sales costs
− Shipping costs
− Omitted marketing costs
− Imputed (fictitious) interest on accounts receivable
+ Intra-company transportation costs
= **Transfer price**

The extent of the omitted cost for internal sales is subject to further specification and expansion (into greater details).

This transfer price corresponds to the **marginal price of the supplying division**. With a given market price, the division is indifferent between internal and external sales at this transfer price, and the whole advantage of internal business is located at the buying division.

Alternatively, the market price could be raised by omitted procurement costs. This corresponds to the **marginal cost of the buying division**. Then the division is indifferent between internal and external purchase, and the whole advantage from the internal business is located at the supplying division.

Interim solutions of these cases are the even split-up of the joint advantages of internal business or a combination of both methods.

Example

The market price amounts to 100. The omitted cost of the supplying division is 5 and for the buying division is 3. The total advantage from internal business (synergistic effect) amounts to $5 + 3 = 8$. They equal the "cost" of the market utilisation.

- Marginal price of the supplying division: $100 - 5 = 95$.
- Marginal price of the buying division: $100 + 3 = 103$.
- Symmetric split-up of the advantage: $100 - 5 + (5 + 3)/2 = 99$.
- Combination of the methods: $100 - 5 + 3 = 98$.

Fundamentally, every transfer price R within the range of $95 \leq R \leq 103$ leads to an incentive for internal transfer for both divisions. The splitting-up of the synergistic effect of 8 is completely arbitrary. In this respect, every modification is equally good or bad, provided that the incentive for internal transfer remains intact. However, the modifications differ about the question of whether it comes to a transfer at all. The previous example of the last section with an imperfect market of the intermediate product would produce a transfer price in the amount of $R = 120 - 16 + 10 = 114$ for a combination of both methods. However, this price lies beyond the identified transfer price interval $104 \leq R \leq 110$ so that Division 2 would reject the supplementary order and would fail the real optimal decision for the company as a whole, which would not be found in a decentralised organisation.

An advantage of the approach of the marginal price of the supplying division can be seen in the fact that it leads to a relatively low transfer price with which the buying division gains a rather large leeway for price setting, which typically is favourable from the perspective of the company as a whole. Another reason for such a modification could lie in the (relatively) lower risk that the supplying division would face.

Setting the transfer price below the market price can impose control effects if the supplying division can act monopolistically against the buying division, for example, to protect intellectual property. This leads to distortions of supply and internal demand for the intermediate product. With the help of a price drop induced by the head office, the distortion, when limited capacity of the supplying division exists, can be reduced. With it, the internal sales volume of the intermediate product is increased with the reverse effect on the amounts of the external sales. This is favourable from the company's view.

Chapter 4
Cost-Based Transfer Prices

Abstract Transfer prices linked to cost figures are most frequently applied in practice. A variety of forms exists and are described in this chapter, including cost-plus, multi-tier, and dual transfer prices. Some of the forms can be shown to fulfill the required functions under the described circumstances.

Keywords Marginal costs · HIRSHLEIFER model · Incentive effects · Full costs · Cost-plus · Opportunity costs · Multi-tier transfer prices · Agency model

Transfer prices linked to cost figures in different ways are most frequently applied in practice. They encompass a relatively diverse group of different transfer price types, namely based on:

- Actual costs or standard (budgeted) costs,
- Marginal costs or full costs,
- Costs or cost "plus" surcharge.

Empirical surveys show that transfer prices based on marginal costs are rather rare and those based on full costs are most frequently in use. At first glance, this is surprising, as can be shown in the following analysis: there are situations in which marginal costs optimally fulfil the **coordination function**, while it is difficult to find situations in which full cost-based transfer prices are optimal. Nevertheless, the following descriptions will also show the pitfalls of the coordination qualities of marginal cost-based transfer prices. This might better explain the aversion towards such transfer prices in practice.

4.1 Actual Costs Versus Standard Costs

Transfer prices determined on the basis of **actual costs** lead to a precise coverage of the supplying division's (reported) costs in each case. However, the purchasing division only knows the transfer price afterwards. Therefore, it carries the whole

P. Schuster, *Transfer Prices and Management Accounting*,
SpringerBriefs in Accounting, DOI 10.1007/978-3-319-14750-5_4

risk of cost variations and must base its operational decisions on expected actual costs. The actual costs often depend on the other divisions' demands as well. The transfer price is not isolating.

Example With increasing units per month, the cost per unit often declines. If a division can adjust (for example delay) its orders within a certain period, it will prefer to buy during the months, during which the other divisions buy in higher numbers.

For transfer prices based on **standard costs** (or budgeted costs), the exact budgeted costs are covered. The difference between standard and actual costs (**cost variances**) affects the result only of the selling division, which carries with it the whole risk. This has the advantage that divisional management has an **incentive** to act economically. In contrast, if all costs are covered anyway by the transfer price (determined ex post), any such incentive largely disappears. Frequently the cost variance consists of a **capacity variance**. Their allocation must be treated in a differentiated way according to its causation, i.e. the reason why it arose. If the purchasing division decides on the amounts and if the supplying division must fulfil the internal demand, the capacity variance has to be allocated to the purchasing division, i.e. the transfer price should be based instead on actual costs. To be able to allocate inefficiencies to the selling division, the transfer price would have to be set on a flexible budget on the basis of the standard cost. If the supplying division has decision power in regard to the amounts and can determine its capacity itself, the capacity variance has to be allocated to them, i.e. the transfer price should equal standard costs.

A potential disadvantage of standard costs lies in the fact that **adaptation decisions** of the purchasing division cannot take place on account of the actual cost change, because the information is not available in time. *Example*: the purchasing division has a substitutive production function. If an input factor purchased internally becomes more expensive, another minimal cost combination arises. If it is settled at standard costs, the division remains with its planned factor combination, although this is not optimal in ex post view.

On the other hand, the **determination of standard costs** requires an additional step: if the divisions agree on standard costs, possibly on the basis of an offer with fixed prices, the supplying division can utilise its better state of knowledge of the real (expected) costs. If the head office determines the standard costs, it will be suddenly involved again in the details of the operational business from which it wanted to free itself by decentralisation; additionally it requires the same level of information as that of the division. Depending on the situation of the head office (i.e. whether the advantages dominate or the disadvantages), it could be meaningful on a cost-benefit basis, to allow head office to set the standard costs for the divisions. A partial allocation of the cost variances could be considered as well.

4.2 Marginal Cost-Based Transfer Price

As can be formally shown, optimum, i.e. profit maximising, decisions from the perspective of the company as a whole, can be found only by marginal costs, understood as relevant costs for short-term decisions. Thus, they solve the coordination problem. However, it is achieved only under very specific conditions in regard to the level and state of information of the head office and divisions and only appears to be solved. The rare use of marginal cost-based transfer prices in practice emphasises this as well.

The Hirshleifer Model

Published in 1956, a paper by HIRSHLEIFER forms the basis of the argumentation and the following example shows the relationships and their effects.

Example Division 1 produces an intermediate product, which is further processed by Division 2 into a marketable final product. There is no market for the intermediate product, or there are supply and purchase limits, which do not allow divisions to use a market for this intermediate product. The processing costs of both divisions amount to:

$$C_1 = 20 + \frac{x^2}{2} \text{ and } C_2 = 2 + x$$

The market for the final product is monopolistic with a price demand function of $p(x) = 16 - x$. Figure 4.1 shows this situation. Both decentralised divisions should determine their output volumes. How high must the transfer price be, so that both divisions decide on identical amounts, which are also optimal from the company's perspective?

The **central solution** as a reference solution is determined by the maximisation of total profit π:

$$\max_x \pi = p(x) \cdot x - C_1(x) - C_2(x)$$

A necessary condition is that the first derivation of the profit according to x equals zero, i.e.

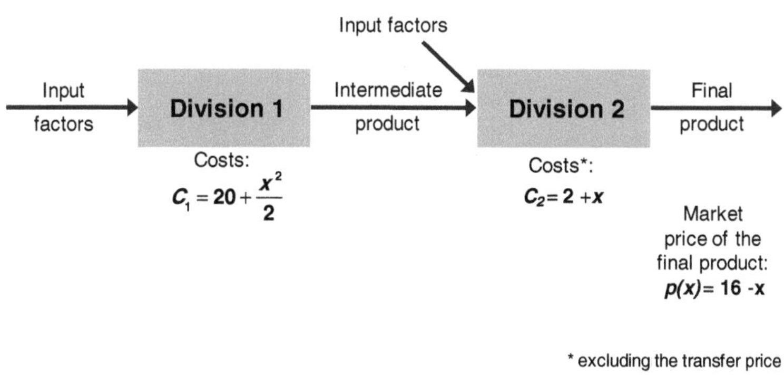

Fig. 4.1 The situation of the HIRSHLEIFER model

$$p(x^*) + p'(x^*) \cdot x^* - C_1'(x^*) - C_2'(x^*) = 0$$

x^* is the optimal (COURNOT) amount that arises for the example as follows:

$$\pi = (16 - x) \cdot x - 20 - \frac{x^2}{2} - 2 - x = -\frac{3x^2}{2} + 15x - 22$$
$$\pi' = -3x + 15 \text{ and } x^* = 5$$

The second derivation is negative. Therefore, this is a maximum (here at the same time the global maximum). The maximum profit amounts to $\pi(x^*) = 5 = 15.5$

Under **decentralised decision-making**, divisional managers independently determine their respective output volumes. Both maximise their divisional profits, taking the transfer price R into account for the transferred intermediate product,

$$\max_x \pi_1 = R \cdot x - C_1(x)$$
$$\max_x \pi_2 = p(x) \cdot x - R \cdot x - C_2(x)$$

The optimal amount in each case depends on the transfer price R. Table 4.1 gives three examples of transfer prices. It is obvious that the transfer price has no influence on the total profit $\pi = \pi_1 + \pi_2$.

There is only one transfer price at which both divisions want to transfer the same amounts. This amount is also optimal from the company's perspective at the same time. This transfer price equals the **marginal cost of the supplying division in the optimum**, namely: $R = C_1'(x^*) = x^* = 5$. The optimal divisional amounts $x_i,\ i = 1, 2$ assuming the maximisation of the decentralised target functions according to the amount x:

Table 4.1 Optimal amounts for different transfer prices

Amount x	2	3	4	5	6	7
Transfer price = 3						
Profit1	-16	**-15.5**	-16	-17.5	-20	-23.5
Profit2	18	25	30	33	**34**	33
Total profit	2	9.5	14	**15.5**	14	9.5
Transfer price = 5						
Profit1	-12	-9.5	-8	**-7.5**	-8	-9.5
Profit2	14	19	22	**23**	22	19
Total profit	2	9.5	14	**15.5**	14	9.5
Transfer price = 7						
Profit1	-8	3.5	0	2.5	4	**4.5**
Profit2	10	13	**14**	13	10	5
Total profit	2	9.5	14	**15.5**	14	9.5

$$\pi_1' = R - C_1'(x) = 5 - x \text{ and } x_1 = 5 = x^*$$
$$\pi_2' = p(x) + p'(x) \cdot x - R - C_2'(x) = 16 - 2x - 5 - 1 \text{ and } x_2 = 5 = x^*$$

Both divisions independently choose $x^* = 5$. There is no other transfer price that leads to the same result.

However, the use of marginal costs as the transfer price solves the coordination problem only apparently. The head office must determine the transfer price $R = 5$, and the question arises of how it could know this transfer price. To be able to determine $R = 5$, it must solve the decision problem. If that problem is solved, the head office might as well stipulate the output volumes to the divisions. Therefore, decentralised decision-making, with an imposed transfer price solves, a false problem.

Additionally, the **profit allocation** of the divisions using a marginal cost-based transfer price is hardly sufficient, i.e. suitable. The **split-up** of total profit is entirely **arbitrary** and typically favours the buying division. Depending on its cost function, the supplying division "gains" only its marginal cost and faces a loss, with a linear cost function in the amount of its fixed costs. If the marginal costs are increasing, the loss becomes lower, or else higher.

Incentive Effects

Assume that the head office only determines how the transfer price should be set, i.e. based on the marginal costs of the supplying division. Then, new **problems** appear: Division 1 and Division 2 have an incentive to behave in a way not desired by the head office. As a consequence, in each case, the coordination function is not fulfilled.

Division 2 will recognise that the transfer price is actually a **function of the amount purchased**, i.e. $R = R(x) = C_1'$, and not merely a constantly given value. It virtually becomes the monopolistic customer. The decision problem changes into

$$\max_x \pi_2 = p(x) \cdot x - R(x) \cdot x - C_2(x)$$
$$\begin{aligned} \pi_2' &= p(x) + p'(x) \cdot x - R(x) - R'(x) \cdot x - C_2'(x) \\ &= 16 - 2x - x - x - 1 = 15 - 4x \end{aligned}$$

The profit-maximising amount is now lower than x^*, namely $x_2 = 3.75$. The divisional profit of Division 2 rises from $\pi_2(x^*) = 23$ to $\pi_2(x_2) = 26.125$. However, from the perspective of the company as a whole, this amount leads to a less favourable situation with a lower total company profit.

Division 1 has to struggle with other problems. First, the delivery of the optimal amount x^* leads to a loss in the amount of $\pi_1(x^*) = -7.5$. This is a **fundamental disadvantage** of the use of marginal cost-based transfer prices: with the exception of the case of strongly increasing marginal costs, Division 1 will always determine **a loss**. Therefore, other activities must guarantee that Division 1 actually produces the intermediate product for the subsequent company divisions.

However, Division 1 often has another choice of reaction in this situation. If its cost function C_1, is only known to itself (**private information**), the head office or Division 2 (depending on who sets the transfer price) must ask Division 1 for this information. Divisional costs can hardly be seen and examined by "strangers". Assume that the division additionally produces other products than the intermediate product in question. As every allocation of fixed costs to individual products is arbitrary to a certain extent, enough leeway remains to distort the cost in one direction or another.

Division 1 can affect the selection of the transfer price by **untruthful information** and with it, the amount purchased and its own divisional profit at the same time. Assume Division 1 reports its cost function as follows:

$$\hat{C}_1 = 20 + \frac{3x^2}{2}$$

It indicates higher variable costs than actually arise. The head office (or the non-monopolistic customer Division 2) then determines:

$$\max_x \pi(\hat{C}_1) = p(x) \cdot x - \hat{C}_1(x) - C_2(x) = 15x - \frac{5x^2}{2} - 22$$

The optimal amount is $\hat{x} = 3$ with the transfer price R

$$\hat{C}_1'(x) = 3x = 9$$

and the profit of Division 1 (π_1) rises to +2.5. This is to the detriment of total company profit and the profit of Division 2.

If the structure of the cost function is known by $C_1 = 20 + \delta \cdot x^2$ and the distortion is limited to the parameter δ, then the above distorted cost information is optimal from the perspective of Division 1 (the reader is invited to check this).

False incentives in regard to decisions about production technology are to be expected, as far as such decisions are made within profit centre responsibilities. The supplying division might oppose such a product technology investment favourable by itself, which leads to higher divisional fixed costs but to lower variable costs. Similar effects appear with investments in human resources, for example, for improvements in staff qualification.

Linear Costs and Revenues

The model shown up to now assumes that divisional profits are strictly concavely dependent upon the amount being transferred internally between the divisions. This was achieved in the example of Division 1 by a convex cost function and for Division 2 by a concave revenue function. In the following example, linear costs and revenues are assumed, and misguidance by the marginal costs is then less likely.

Example Division 1 produces an intermediate product, which is processed in Division 2 into a final product and sold in the external market. The sales price p is constant, and the cost functions are linear:

$$C_i(x) = C_i^F + c_i \cdot x \quad \text{for } i = 1, 2$$

In order to limit the solution, there must be a limited resource or bottleneck in at least one division. For each of the two divisions, (potentially effective) restrictions are assumed in the following way:

$$\upsilon_i \cdot x \leq \bar{V}_i \quad \text{for } i = 1, 2$$

The consumption of one output unit, υ_i, uses the limited resource and $\bar{V}_i$ equals the available units of that resource (e.g. time, machine-hours) in division i.

Division 1 decides as follows:

$$\max_x \pi_1 = R \cdot x - C_1^F - c_1 \cdot x$$

The solution is:

$$x_1 = \begin{cases} 0 & \text{for } R < C_1 \\ \frac{\bar{V}_1}{\upsilon_1} & \text{for } R \geq C_1 \end{cases}$$

Analogously, it applies for Division 2 (the condition $x_2 = \bar{V}_2/\upsilon_2$ is: $R \leq p - c_2$). Assuming that both divisions must choose an equal amount so that it finally arises from $x^* = \min\{x_1, x_2\}$.

The **optimal solution** from the company perspective is identical to the **decentralised solution** when

1. $p - c_1 - c_2 \geq 0$ (production is profitable), and
2. $c_1 \leq R \leq p - c_2$ (the transfer price guarantees that both divisions will produce).

The head office must not know the restrictions, just as it typically is sufficient to possess only an approximate knowledge of the variable cost amounts, to fulfil the coordination function. The reason lies in the fact that the optimal solution reacts relatively insensitively concerning the underlying measures; this was not the case in the previous example. If the transfer price is set exactly at the marginal cost of the supplying division ($c_1 \leq R$), this insensitivity is partly lost again.

Marginal Costs at the Limit of Capacity

Marginal costs have to be modified at the **capacity limits**. Assume that Division 1 not only produces the intermediate product needed by Division 2 but also sells other products to divisions or to the market, and it has now reached its capacity limit. Then, the transfer price must include the direct variable costs as well as the

opportunity costs of the bottleneck, i.e. the contribution margin crowded out by production of the intermediate product. If Division 1 only reaches its capacity limit by the internal demand of the intermediate product, the transfer price jumps from the original marginal costs to the new marginal costs (including the opportunity costs).

Then, taking the borderline case of the marginal costs equalling the **market price**: if a market exists for the intermediate product and if Division 1 has the possibility of selling the product at the market price, then this market price equals the relevant revenue measure for the determination of the opportunity costs in a bottleneck situation.

If the producing division decides its capacity, **false incentives** can arise: the producing division is interested in a high transfer price and knows that the transfer price will rise in line with a shortage of the capacity. Therefore, it might have the incentive to choose a capacity too small.

Vice versa, the buying divisions, during the budgeting phase, are inclined to overestimate their demand. Thereby, the producing division is pushed toward a high(er) capacity, and the probability of underutilisation rises.

4.3 Full Cost-Based Transfer Price

The basic idea of full cost-based transfer prices consists of the idea that the producing division (on average) should be reimbursed to the amount of their **total** (or **full**) **costs**. The producing division is then not threatened by a loss, in contrast to the situation when marginal costs are the basis of transfer prices. Yet, the producing division does not achieve a profit, and the company profit appears at the purchasing division. With it, an arbitrary **split-up of the total company profit** is again visible.

Sometimes **combined transfer price systems** of the type where full costs are covered are found in practice, limited to the market price, if it is lower. The consequence for the profit allocation function is the fact that the producing division not only cannot reach a profit situation but often faces a loss described by the difference between full costs and market price. This increases the pressure on the division to produce less expensively; however, it does not lead to a divisional profit.

Transfer prices on a full cost basis are very **popular** in **company practice**. Strictly speaking, this means every company practically has one transfer price system applied in a simple way, i.e. without further considerations, as it can be based on their cost accounting system, with little further adjustments.

In practice, the allocation of overhead costs is often excused and explained by the argument of creating cost awareness in divisional managers. As a rule, total costs are far higher than variable costs; if only the latter were charged, divisional managers might get the impression that production costs are (too) small. The transfer price based on full costs should create an incentive to behave in a "cost-aware" manner.

A major argument for the extensive refusal of marginal cost-based transfer prices in practice, and for favouring full cost-based transfer prices, is that an internal production of intermediate products rarely is done with only a short-term perspective. Therefore, the usual argument, that only marginal costs fulfil the coordination function generally cannot be valid, as this is only applied to short-term decisions on account of the definition of marginal costs. For **long-term decisions**, the use of marginal costs is unsuitable as a decision criterion; rather, relevant measures encompass all changes caused by the decision. However, typically full costs are similarly unsuitable for it because:

1. Full costs encompass all costs, but it depends on the decision problem as to which cost components are relevant.
2. Full costs are often subject to variances according to **capacity utilisation** of the producing division. This can be avoided by the use of budgeted capacity instead of actual capacity utilisation for the determination of full costs. Yet, this can lead to false incentives in the budgeting process.
3. If several products are produced by the producing division and only part of them are supplied internally, the well-known problem of the **overhead costs' allocation** to products arises. This is largely solved **arbitrarily**, and with it, the full costs of the internal products are arbitrary as well.

If decisions are to be made on the basis of costs rather than on cash outflows (as in investment appraisal), full costs can form a simplified **approximation** of the costs that are changeable by the decision in the **long-term** view.

The allocation of fixed costs, however, becomes necessary when the fixed costs can be influenced. *Example*: the head office considers investments in continuing education. The investment causes one time fixed costs, and as a result, a reduction of direct costs for a certain percentage arises in the divisions. The head office does not precisely know the savings potential of the divisions. Unless the costs of the investment were not charged, every division would have an incentive to exaggerate this savings potential, as it only would gain advantages but not costs of this investment. Therefore, from an ex ante perspective, the (later) fixed costs must be contained in the transfer price.

The inclusion of fixed costs in the transfer price also serves to control the **demand for limited resources**.

Example A company acquires the authorisation to use a literature database. The monthly fee is 1,000 and includes 100 min of database searches each month. A "normal" inquiry in this database is charged at 30 per minute. How can the costs per minute be allocated to the internal divisions using the database?

At the beginning of the month, the number of minutes used for searches is not rateable. The marginal costs of the first 100 min amount to 0, the marginal costs of every exceeding minute to 30. If the transfer price is set at the marginal costs, the divisions will carelessly handle it, and only once 100 min are used, do they incur costs and this has to be compared to the benefit of further searches. The control effects are diminishing if the principle "Who comes first, gets it free first" is applied. It might occur that the benefit of a search equals 5 per minute and is only used because the search is (still) free. A search is considered as a virtually free resource. A search after the 100 min are used and which perhaps leads to benefits of 25 per minute would not be done, just because it happens later in the month.

It is not necessarily optimal to immediately charge the divisions 30 per minute, because it might be that the 100 min are not exhausted and, therefore, the marginal costs actually amount to 0.

Raising the price for the use of a resource **lessens the demand**. In the ideal case, the capacity is exactly utilised; its respective costs are the **opportunity costs** that can hardly be estimated in the reality of company practice. Opportunity costs can consist of:

- Costs of delays: costs as a result of the delayed fulfilment. *Example*: maintenance costs.
- Costs of quality deterioration: *Example*: because of work overload in the legal department, the quality drops or the work duration rises.
- Costs of procurement from other sources or own production. *Example*: installation of its own legal department instead of hiring an external lawyer.

The allocation of full costs in such situations can represent a simple and economically justified attempt to **approximate** the undeterminable opportunity costs of centrally provided services. The quality of this approximation depends on the cost function and the (budgeted and actual) demand for the products. For certain assumptions, the quality of the approximation can be analysed.

Coordination Function

The transfer price on the basis of full costs contains variable costs and fixed costs components and possibly even parts of the profits of the producing division. All these are seen by the buying division entirely as variable costs. They do not only appear as such but actually are variable: if one unit less is purchased, the costs decrease exactly by the amount of the transfer price. This can lead to **incorrect**, i.e. **suboptimal decisions** in decision situations that require the use of variable costs. An example is a one-off special order as shown in the following insertion.

Example

A product is processed in two independent production divisions.

Variable costs (per copy) of Division 1	10
Proportionate fixed costs of Division 1	15
Transfer price (supply from Division 1 to 2)	25
Variable costs (per copy) of Division 2	6
Proportionate fixed costs of Division 2	9
Total costs per copy	40

Cost structure per copy (with given capacity in both divisions):

	Actual		Division 2's perspective	
Variable costs	16	40.0 %	31	77.5 %
Proportionate fixed costs	24	60.0 %	9	22.5 %
Total costs per copy	40	100.0 %	40	100.0 %

A supplementary order at a price of 30 would be rejected by Division 2 although it produces a positive contribution margin of 14 (ca. 47 %).

In addition, effects on the suitability of certain **cost accounting systems** can arise, depending on the cost structure, namely the relation of the variable and fixed costs. If the real cost structure is distorted by transfer prices, a company can apply an unsuitable cost accounting system without recognising it. For example, due to the data, the company might believe that a high proportion of the product costs are direct costs and a change toward another cost accounting system, which would trace the indirect costs more precisely, is not economical. Distortions and incorrect decisions grow due to the less suitable cost accounting system in use.

4.4 Multi-tier Transfer Prices

Two-tier transfer prices split the transfer price into two parts:

- The current products are charged at **marginal costs**.
- Additionally, a **single amount** is charged in each period.

With this suggestion, the **characteristics** of marginal cost-based transfer prices remain intact for the (short-term) decision-making. However, the disadvantage of the marginal costs imposing losses at the producing division is reduced or avoided by the single periodic payment. This single amount can be interpreted as a charge for the supply or reservation of the producing division's capacity.

It leads to the reporting of fixed costs, yet remains **decision-neutral** in the short-term perspective, in contrast to the full costs approach. In view of the single payment, two-tier transfer prices are only meaningful for long-term transfer relations.

Two-tier transfer prices are rarely applied in the reality of company practice. However, certain market services (for example, electricity and telephone services) are charged in this way. In principle, this corresponds to the approach of a flexible budget.

In regard to the fixed amount, considerable **flexibility** exists; it can be determined to cover budgeted or actual fixed costs. To induce an incentive to the producing division for determining the optimal capacity it is possible to only charge the costs of utilisation (capacity costs of the budgeted capacity utilisation). The amount due might also contain a profit surcharge.

If the fixed amount is interpreted as covering the capacity reserved, the question arises how to treat short-term **variances** from the budgeted capacity utilisation.

Example Two purchasing divisions reserve full capacity with 30 and 70 %, respectively; they pay accordingly 30,000 and 70,000 to the producing division. By the end of the planning period, Division 1 still has 10 % of its capacity available and will not need them. Presumably, Division 2 has fully exhausted its reserved capacities. Now Division 2 gets a supplementary order that needs 5 % of the capacity. Division 2 has no available capacity while there is still free capacity available (and will not otherwise be used). How should they proceed now?

Because the capacity will probably not be useable otherwise from an ex post perspective, Division 2 should receive it free of charge. The capacity costs are sunk costs and should not affect the decision about the supplementary order. If Division 2 had to buy the required capacity from Division 1 at a price of, for example, 5,000, this amount would suddenly become relevant for the decision. This could lead to the supplementary order being rejected, despite being profitable from the perspective of the company as a whole.

Yet, if a division can receive capacity free of charge afterwards, it will have an **incentive** to initially reserve a capacity too small (in tendency). Once the division exceeds the original reserved capacity, it receives additional capacity free of charge as long as there is some capacity left. This can be examined further in the capacity decision of the producing division: if there is too small a demand announced in the budgeting phase, the producing division will install too small a capacity, and the total capacity of the company as a whole could then be too low.

Whether the advantages of two-tier transfer prices in comparison to marginal cost- and full cost-based transfer prices outweigh their disadvantages, must be judged individually.

4.5 Full Cost Plus Profit Surcharge as a Transfer Price

The transfer price must not always cover only just the costs of the producing division; it can also contain a profit share, particularly in industries in which orders to cost plus a profit surcharge (cost plus) are calculated. From the perspective of the producing division, this procedure provides equal treatment of an internal buyer with a regular external customer.

The essential motivation to include a profit surcharge in the transfer price results from the **profit allocation function**. In the suggested way, the producing division can also achieve a profit. However, as already shown, every kind of profit split-up is arbitrary when synergies exist. The main problem of cost plus profit surcharge as a transfer price is finding the "appropriate" profit surcharge. The following **possibilities** can be used:

- A percentage of the full costs,
- An appropriate interest charge on capital tied-up (return on capital),
- By negotiation between the divisions.

Frequently a lower profit surcharge is assumed for the internal buyers than for external customers, but again every profit surcharge is arbitrary in this sense.

From the perspective of the **coordination function**, full costs plus profit surcharge are not necessarily suitable. All arguments against the use of full costs again apply, such as the risk of incorrect decisions or the distortion of the cost structure.

False incentives result from the split-up of a jointly earned profit, if a division can improve the profit situation by individual activities. Due to the fact that the costs are recorded in his division while profit is shared with other divisions, activities might not be executed that are profitable from the perspective of the company as a whole. For example, every cost reduction activity with a proportional profit surcharge ceteris paribus leads to a decrease of the absolute profit amount.

An Agency Model

The following part shows a situation in which full cost plus transfer prices provide the optimum solution and solve the underlying **coordination problem**. An agency model shows two sequential intertwined divisions (Fig. 4.2).

The following situation is given (see in details Wagenhofer 1992; the underlying model type was first examined by Sappington 1983): Division 1 produces an intermediate product which is processed further by Division 2. It is sold at the market where a perfect competition situation exists and at a market price of p. The variable production costs in Division 1 are severely convex in the production volume x. Furthermore, the costs depend on the "type" of manager, i.e. $C_1 = C_1(x, \theta)$, and on the parameter θ. The type describes the expertise of the manager; it can

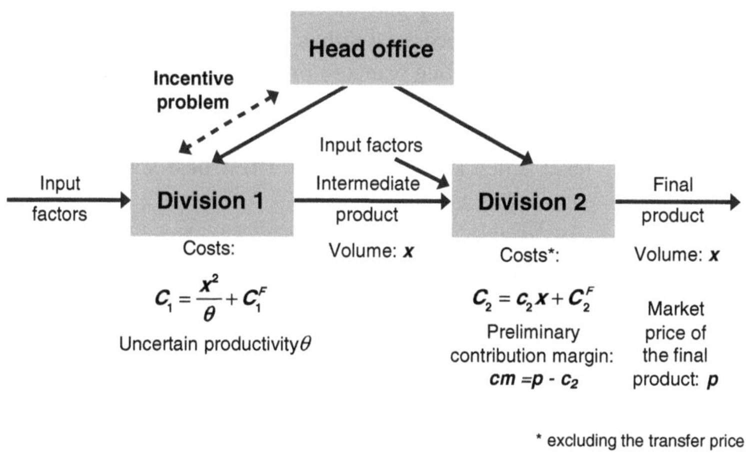

Fig. 4.2 The organisational structure in an agency model

also register the special production conditions in Division 1. The manager of Division 1 precisely knows his type. On the contrary, the head office only has a priori expectations about it. A higher θ leads to a decrease of the production costs for any amount of x. The cost function is:

$$C_1(x, \theta) = \frac{x}{\theta} + C_1^F$$

Only two types may be realistic, $\theta = 1$ (low productivity) or $\theta = 2$ (high productivity). The probability of both types is 50 % in each case.

The subsequent processing and sales costs in Division 2 are linearly related to the amount x with $C_2 = c_2 \cdot x + C_2^F$. The preliminary contribution margin (without the costs of the input factor bought from Division 1) $cm = p - c_2$ is assumed to equal 1 to simplify matters. In regard to Division 2 where no asymmetric information exists, the head office needs no indirect coordination instruments, such as a transfer price, to control the division. Therefore, Division 2 can be omitted from the following analysis, and the head office indirectly takes over their business relations with Division 1.

The manager of Division 1 is risk-neutral. To motivate him to collaborate, the head office must offer him at least as much remuneration as he would receive elsewhere (**reservation utility**). It is assumed that the divisional manager receives the full divisional profit (alternatively, non-monetary utilities, such as praise, trust, power, etc.). The reservation utility is assumed to equal $-C_1^F$ (thus, the transfer price must only cover the variable production costs). This must be guaranteed for every type.

A potential **false control** effect can result from the fact that the manager can report to be type $\theta = 1$, although actually being type $\theta = 2$. If the head office can observe the costs afterwards, he only needs to use the difference between actual variable production costs $(x^2/2)$ of x and the required variable costs being type $\theta = 1 \cdot (x^2/2)$ to use for other unnecessary things (such as business trips, customer visits, company cars). The head office wants to prevent this, through the use of the transfer price.

For a better comparison, the solution is determined first with symmetry of information, i.e. the head office knows the type θ (**first best solution**). The head office maximises:

$$\max_x \pi = cm \cdot x - \frac{x^2}{\theta} = x - \frac{x^2}{\theta}$$

for $\theta = 1, 2$; $cm = 1$. The fixed costs are not relevant and, therefore, are not considered. The necessary condition of the first order is: $1 - 2x/\theta = 0$, and the optimal amount x^* depends on θ.

$$x^*(\theta = 1) = 1/2 \text{ and } x^*(\theta = 2) = 1$$

Now the head office could impose the amount appropriate for every type θ, and with it, the imposing of a transfer price itself is not necessary. If the head office determines a transfer price, it could be made dependent upon x and θ, i.e.

$R = R(x, \theta)$. The amount of the transfer prices would need to acknowledge the **reservation utility** of the manager:

$$\pi_1 = R(x,\theta) \cdot x - \frac{x^2}{\theta} - C_1^F \geq -C_1^F \text{ or } R(x,\theta) \cdot x - \frac{x^2}{\theta} \geq 0$$

for every θ. The lowest transfer price just fulfils this in equation, i.e. $R(x, \theta) = x/\theta$. From it arises $R(0.5; 1) = 0.5$, $R(1; 2) = 0.5$ and $R(x, \theta) \leq 0$ (sanctions) for other (x, θ) combinations ($R = 0$ is a sufficient sanction because for each $R \leq 0$ every type θ the amount $x = 0$ is chosen). It is assumed that the manager, in the case of indifference, produces the amount desired by the head office). By coincidence the transfer prices are identical in the example for both types; normally it depends on θ.

In the case of **asymmetric information**, the transfer price can only depend on the amount x but not on the type θ, as it is unknown to the head office. To determine the transfer price $R(x)$ the head office maximises the expected profit (before fixed costs and with $cm = 1$),

$$\max_x E[\pi] = \sum_{\theta=1}^{2} \frac{1}{2} \cdot [x_\theta - R(x_\theta) \cdot x_\theta]$$

The amount x_θ equals the amount reported by the manager on account of his respective type θ with the following equation:

$$\max_x \pi_1 = R(x) \cdot x - \frac{x^2}{\theta} - C_1^F \quad \text{for } \theta = 1, 2$$

Furthermore, the head office must guarantee that the divisional manager will at least receive his reservation utility independent of his respective type θ:

$$\pi_1(x_\theta, \theta) = R(x_\theta) \cdot x_\theta - \frac{x_\theta^2}{\theta} - C_1^F \geq -C\frac{F}{1} \quad \text{for } \theta = 1, 2 \quad \text{or}$$

$$R(x_1) \cdot x_1 - x_1^2 \geq 0$$

$$R(x_2) \cdot x_2 - x_2^2 \geq 0$$

This problem can be solved by a LAGRANGE approach. A deeper analysis of the **solution structure** is achieved by the above listed condition: a type $\theta = 1$ manager will certainly have no incentive to imitate a type $\theta = 2$ manager, i.e. to produce x_2 instead of x_1. Therefore, only the reverse case must be considered, namely:

$$R(x_2) \cdot x_2 - \frac{x_2^2}{2} \geq R(x_1) \cdot x_1 - \frac{x_1^2}{2} = R(x_1) \cdot x_1 - x_1^2 + \frac{x_1^2}{2} > R(x_1) \cdot x_1 - x_1^2 \geq 0$$

In this case a type $\theta = 2$ manager receives more than his reservation utility, i.e. achieves a **productivity gain** that is actually caused by the asymmetric information.

Certainly, the head office could insist on the fact that *every* type produces just the first best amount. However, this would mean a relatively high payment to a type

$\theta = 2$ manager. Therefore, it is preferable to impose a **lower amount** on a type $\theta = 1$ manager, which would result in lower costs to prevent a type $\theta = 2$ manager from imitating a type $\theta = 1$, and still producing the optimal, higher amount.

The solution of this model (**second best solution**) is as follows: a manager with high productivity ($\theta = 2$) is motivated to produce the optimal amount $x_2 = x^*(\theta = 2) = 1$; a manager with low productivity $\theta = 1$ produces a lower amount, namely $x_1 = 1/3 < 1/2 = x(\theta = 1)$. Production is lower than in case of symmetric information, the head office must also pay less to the manager. Actually, the **transfer price** must be determined for both amounts x_1 and x_2, and amounts to:

$$R(x_1) = \frac{1}{3} \text{ and } R(x_2) = \frac{5}{9}$$

The head office can prevent other amounts from being chosen by sufficient sanctions (for example, $R(x) = 0$ for $x \neq x_1, x_2$). A manager of the type $\theta = 2$ is indifferent between the two amounts:

$$\pi_1(x_2, 2) = \frac{5}{9} \cdot 1 - \frac{1}{2} - C_1^F = \frac{1}{3} \cdot \frac{1}{3} - \frac{1}{18} - C_1^F = \pi_1(x_1, 2)$$

and it can be assumed that he then chooses case x_2. On the contrary, a type $\theta = 1$ strictly prefers x_1:

$$\pi_1(x_1, 1) = \frac{1}{3} \cdot \frac{1}{3} - \frac{1}{9} - C_1^F = -C_1^F > \frac{5}{9} \cdot 1 - 1 - C_1^F = \pi_1(x_2, 1)$$

As a result the divisional managers reveal their **real type** (in a consideration of multiple periods, this must not necessarily be the most favourable choice). The type $\theta = 1$ manager receives his alternative utility ($-C_1^F$), and a type $\theta = 2$ manager the same plus an additional 1/18. Therefore, both will have an interest in cooperation. The solution can provide interesting insights into cost-based transfer pricing arguments and shows the following **characteristics**:

- The optimal transfer price covers the **average costs**, i.e. not the marginal costs, of production. In addition, the reservation utility of the divisional manager must be guaranteed. Therefore, it can contain a profit share, which is required to lead the manager to collaborate (due to the simplistic assumptions in the model, this is not explicitly expressed and shown).
- For the more productive division, the transfer price also contains a **profit share** (reward). This is necessary for the motivation of a more productive manager.
- A **market price** for the intermediate product, if it existed, would interfere in fulfilling the coordination function, as long as it cannot be used by Division 1. If Division 1 could supply externally, the market price would retrieve the function of a lowest limit of the transfer price. However, this was not explicitly included in the described model.

In the above simple model, all decision-makers are risk-neutral. Even if this is not the case, the transfer price can also fulfil a risk-sharing function.

The same solution structure arises even if **asymmetric information** is assumed in other divisions. The **optimal transfer price** strongly depends on the individual division's as well the manager's circumstances, and the coordination can be induced by the head office similar to the procedure of dual transfer prices (see below). However, implementation difficulties can arise when two divisions make arrangements that improve their situation to the detriment of the head office.

Naturally such a simple model does not solve the problems connected with the approach of full costs in company practice. It has a more **conceptual character** and serves for gaining an understanding of the relationship between coordination and assessment function, as well as on transfer prices which cover the costs and contain a profit surcharge.

However, the coordination by means of transfer prices in this situation is not the only possibility. The head office could ask the manager of Division 1 for a **report on his type** θ and then impose the production amounts on the basis of the report, whose accuracy cannot be directly examined by the head office. Yet, the head office can induce incentives for truthful reporting of the manager.

4.6 Dual Transfer Prices

Dual transfer prices (sometimes called "dual-rate transfer prices") make use of an optional variation of internal "prices" unconsidered in the previous discussion: why must the same transfer price be applied to the supplying and purchasing division? Dual transfer prices set **different transfer prices** for the divisions. The head office fulfils a balancing function for the different profits.

Example Division 1 produces an intermediate product at costs of $C_1 = 10 + x^2$. Division 2 processes it further and sells it as a final product at the market for a constant price of $p = 20$. Its costs are $C_2 = 2 + 2x$. Figure 4.3 shows the situation. As a reference, the central solution arises by maximisation of the total profit:

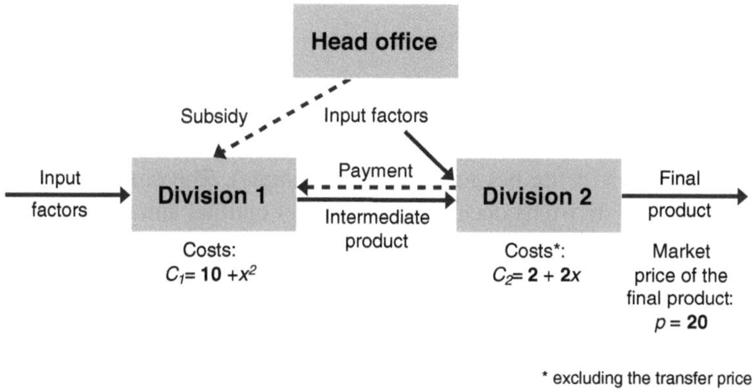

Fig. 4.3 Dual transfer prices

$$\max_x \pi = 20x - (10 + x^2) - (2 + 2x) = -x^2 + 18x - 12$$

Setting the first derivation $\pi' = -2x + 18$ to zero leads to the optimal amount $\pi^* = 9$. The total profit from the transaction amounts to $\pi = 69$.

The **procedure** for the determination of dual transfer prices is the following (this is a simplified suggestion based on Ronen and McKinney 1970):

1. The head office requires information about the (full) costs for different demands of Division 1. In the example, these are

$$c_1 = \frac{C_1(x)}{x} = x + \frac{10}{x}$$

   This equals the transfer price R_2, at which Division 2 procures the intermediate product.
2. The head office requires Division 2's preliminary contribution margins cm_2 (excluding the costs of the intermediate product) for different volumes of the intermediate product. In the example, these are

$$cm_2 = \frac{CM_2}{x} = 20 - 2 - \frac{2}{x} = 18 - \frac{2}{x}.$$

   This becomes the transfer price R_1, for which Division 1 sells the intermediate product internally.

The decentralised decisions with these transfer prices amount to:
Division 1:

$$\max_x \pi_1 = R_1 \cdot x - C_1(x) = \left(18 - \frac{2}{x}\right) \cdot x - 10 - x^2 = -x^2 + 18x - 12$$

Division 2:

$$\max_x \pi_2 = 20x - R_2 \cdot x - C_2(x) = 20x - \left(x + \frac{10}{x}\right) \cdot x - 2 - 2x$$
$$= -x^2 + 18x - 12$$

The divisional profit functions are **identical** to the total profit function of the company (as shown at the beginning of the example). Therefore, independently of each other, both divisions decide the (centrally) optimal amount $x^* = 9$. As an advantage of dual transfer prices, it can be seen that Division 1 gets closer to the market (of the final product) to a certain extent, because achievable contribution margins are imposed as the transfer price. On the other hand, Division 2 has to use a transfer price that corresponds to the intermediate product's production costs. Although the transfer price contains unitised fixed costs, they cease because of the multiplication of the amount and, therefore, are again not relevant for the decision (Fig. 4.4).

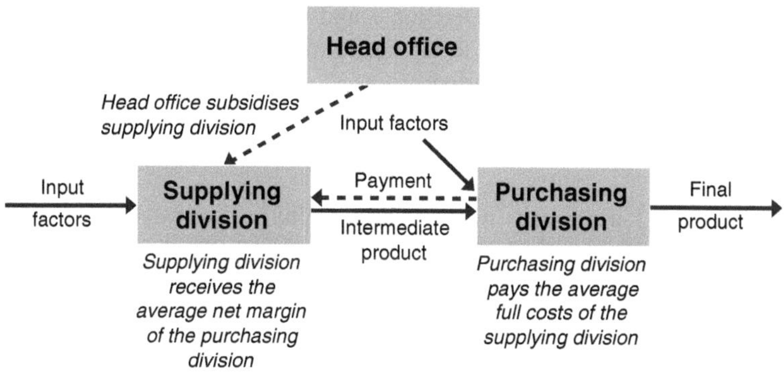

Fig. 4.4 Suggestion for dual transfer prices

The head office must balance the **difference** between the two transfer prices R_1 and R_2. Division 1 receives $R_1 \cdot x = 18x - 2 = 160$, while Division 2 only pays $R_2 \cdot x = x^2 + 10 = 91$. The difference of 69 is covered by the head office and virtually forms a **loss balance**. With it, the total profit of the company cannot be determined as the sum of the divisional profits ($\pi_1 + \pi_2$). The head office always suffers a loss exactly in the amount of the total company profit as a result of the transaction. This is obvious because both divisions maximise the same profit function, and that is why every division achieves a profit of 69, despite the fact that this profit only results once. With transfer price types using identical transfer prices for both divisions, the divisional profits always equals the sum to the total profit. Now the total profit corresponds to the sum of the divisional profits including the loss balance of the head office.

An essential problem consists of the fact that both divisions determine the same profit in the amount of the total company profit, independent of how well they have worked. Ordering the divisions, for example, according to their profitability, is impossible now, i.e. the **profit allocation function** obviously cannot be fulfilled by dual transfer prices. This consequence is one of the principal reasons why dual transfer prices are hardly used in practice and face a **low rate of acceptability**. It also suffers from the fact that two transfer prices for an identical product exist and the question emerges again, which one is the "correct" price? Every answer to it remains unsatisfactory to a certain extent.

Incentive Effects

Dual transfer prices can provide incentives for **distorted information** during the determination of the transfer prices. If one division deviates from its actual cost function, different amounts arise, so that it becomes obvious that one of the two divisions has supplied incorrect cost information. Therefore, it does not lie in the interest of the divisions to individually report incorrectly. However, this is different when the divisions make collusive **arrangements** between them, as they can coordinate the amount through this.

Continuation of the example: Division 1 and Division 2 arrange for Division 1 to report a distorted cost function to the head office. Instead of $c_1 = x + 10/x$, the following cost information is reported:

$$\hat{c}_1 = 0.8x + \frac{10}{x}$$

With it, Division 2 maximises its divisional profits $\pi_2 = 18x - 2 - (0.8x^2 + 10)$ with an optimal amount of 11.25. Therefore, it must "adapt" its cost report in a way that Division 1 also determines the same amount. This is achieved by the following contribution margin per unit function:

$$c\hat{m}_2 = 22.5 - \frac{2}{x}$$

Division 1 maximises $\pi_1 = 22.5x - 2 - (10 + x^2)$ and an optimal amount of 11.25 arises from it.

This **arrangement** is **preferred** by both divisions against truthful reporting of costs: the profit of Division 1 rises from 69 to 114.5625 and of Division 2 from 69 to 89.25. The head office loses by the arrangement between the divisions because of the non-optimal amount, and the total profit falls from $\pi(x = 9) = 69$ to $\pi(x = 11.25) = 63.9375$. In addition, both divisions have higher shares of profits so that the loss balance of the head office grows to $114.5625 + 89.25 - 63.9375 = 139.875$

The only consolation for the head office is that the divisions will find it difficult to agree on an equally favourable solution within the range of credible cost functions under certain circumstances. For example, why should Division 1 achieve a higher advantage from the arrangement than Division 2?

As the internal transfers duplicate the profit from the perspective of both divisions, reduced incentives for efforts searching more favourable **external options** arise and arrangements between the divisions may prevent the use of such superior external offers.

Other suggestions for dual transfer prices exist. A model by Zverovich and Schuster (2015) suggests a combination of a single cost-plus transfer price and the pragmatic process of negotiation and assumes non-linear net average revenue curves. In particular, typical quadratic functions are considered and corresponding transfer price schedules are determined. It is shown that a similar technique can be used for the transfer pricing problem with any net average revenue curve. A similar approach for a more simple revenue function was considered by Tomkins (1990).

Chapter 5
Negotiated Transfer Prices

Abstract Transfer prices as the result of negotiations between the divisions involved in the internal transfer of goods and services are the last type examined. They provide the maximum autonomy to the divisions. A multiplicity of conflicts between the managers may be raised by their use. This chapters also looks at a NASH negotiation solution of the problem.

Keywords Negotiation · Zone of potential agreement · NASH negotiation solution · Hold up model · Risk sharing · Stackelberg solution · Monopoly price

5.1 Effects from Negotiated Transfer Prices

The head office can refrain from determining transfer prices and leave it to the divisions to agree on transfer prices that they find acceptable. Then, transfer prices are the result of negotiations between the divisions involved in the internal transfer of goods and services. However, as a prerequisite for this, the divisions must have the right to refuse internal business. If the internal transfer were imposed, it would be unclear what the negotiations are about, as no division could really threaten with retreat, i.e. to refuse internal transfers; and an arbitrary split-up of the joint profit would be the result.

In the reality of company practice, it must be distinguished whether the negotiation is made on an **ad hoc basis** with no advance planning for each transaction as it arises, or whether the divisions agree **generally** based on certain principles of how the transfer price can be determined in each individual case. The decision about that largely depends in essence on the extent of the internal transactions. The more often it takes place, the more suitable is a general determination. Cost-based transfer prices and particularly market-based transfer prices are often applied for this. The negotiation of general determinations is based on average, expected circumstances, while the case-wise negotiation strongly considers the **specific situation**.

P. Schuster, *Transfer Prices and Management Accounting*,
SpringerBriefs in Accounting, DOI 10.1007/978-3-319-14750-5_5

Negotiated transfer prices provide the **maximum autonomy** to the divisions, and this has advantages and disadvantages. They can act more independent and there is a resulting high **motivation**. Another advantage is that divisions often possess a **much better state of information** about the mutual costs or revenue situation than the head office, so they can make better decisions than if they were confronted with a transfer price set by the "misinformed" head office.

On the other hand, it enables the divisions to make decisions that are optimal for them, but not necessarily for the whole company. If the result of the negotiations is a transfer price other than the one that fulfils the **coordination function** as well as possible, it leads to incorrect decisions from the perspective of the company as a whole. Almost always will the outcome of the negotiations lie somewhere between the costs of the producing division and the contribution margin of the buying division. Therefore, the head office will only find it meaningful to leave the determination of the transfer price at the disposal of the divisions if the advantages outweigh the disadvantages.

Influence Factors on the Negotiation's Results

An agreement between the divisions on the transfer price only takes place if the internal transaction brings both divisions an advantage compared to the **best alternative to a negotiated agreement (BATNA)**. Therefore, the said alternatives determine the **zone of potential agreement (ZOPA)**. The better the alternative options, the smaller the range of outcomes within which the negotiations can lie.

Example: Division 1 and Division 2 negotiate the transfer price of a copy of a product that Division 2 would like to buy from Division 1. The marginal costs of Division 1 amounts to 120, the sales price of the final product produced by Division 2 is 200 and the marginal costs of the completion amounts to 30. Therefore, the preliminary contribution margin equals $200 - 30 = 170$. Assume that the divisions have no alternatives so that the ZOPA lies between [120, 170]. If Division 1 could sell its product to another customer for only 145, the delivery to Division 2 would cause opportunity costs of $145 - 120 = 25$. The ZOPA then shrinks to [145, 170].

Assume now that Division 2 would also have an alternative to purchase the product from **another supplier** at 160, then the ZOPA further decreases to [145, 160]. If Division 2 could externally buy the product even at 140, then there would no longer be a ZOPA, and both divisions would follow their alternatives. However, this would be favoured by the perspective of the head office because the sum of the divisional profits then amounts to $(145 - 120) + (170 - 140) = 55$ compared to $170 - 120 = 50$ for the case of an internal transaction. Figure 5.1 presents the changes of the ZOPA for the described example.

A division is a priori favoured by the existence of **strong alternatives** because it shifts the limits of the transfer price in a direction favourable for the division. Therefore, both divisional managers will try to find suitable alternatives, for example, by obtaining external offers. However, in the reality of company practice, it is often difficult to find externals who take part in such a game, if only now and then an order results. In practice, for standard products often a part of the amount to be procured will be kept internally and the other part for that reason externally.

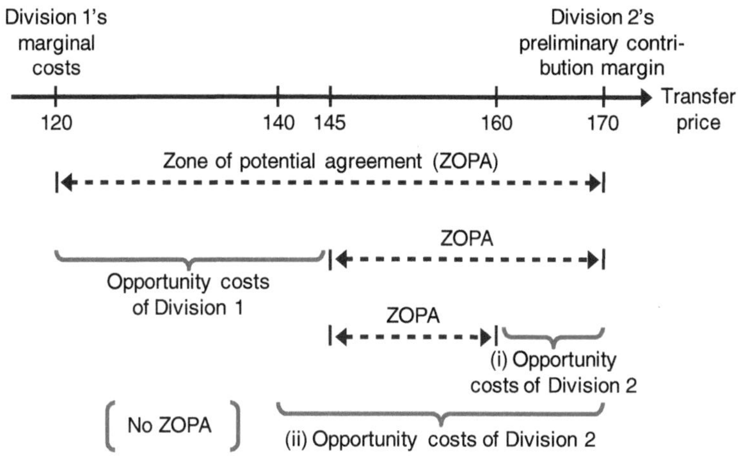

Fig. 5.1 Zone of potential agreement

However, **within the zone of potential agreement** the negotiations' outcome is hardly predictable; it depends on the situation and individual circumstances. Negotiating power (on account of better alternatives) plays an essential role. Other effects such as time pressure, stress, etc., and particularly different individual negotiating skills of the divisional manager, influence the transfer price. The more "skilful" manager can further influence the transfer price. Certainly, negotiating skill is an important manager quality; however, the divisional profit should instead measure the economic viability of the production, and this is sometimes overlooked.

Remark

There is possibly no single accounting topic that consumes more management time and energy in multi-profit centre companies than the business of establishing acceptable transfer prices. The expenditure of energy in this division far exceeds that expended on pricing products sold to outside customers (Seed quoted in Thomas, 1980, p. 117).

Negotiated transfer prices have the **disadvantage** that negotiations can raise a multiplicity of **conflicts** between the managers of a company. This can negatively influence the "climate" in a company and endanger the necessary co-operation of divisional managers. In addition, negotiations are often very **time-consuming**.

Conflicts between divisions An empirical questionnaire survey of 84 large U.S. companies (Lambert 1979) brought the following results:

1. Negotiated transfer prices lead to significantly larger conflicts than cost-based or market-based transfer prices.
2. The conflicts are stronger if the divisions cannot use an external market.

It is meaningful to agree on a **conciliation procedure** in advance. The divisions can probably more easily agree on such a procedure at a time during which the actual circumstances are not yet obvious than later on with a certain outcome of the negotiations. Alternatively, the head office can suggest such a conciliation procedure to intervene in the negotiation process. It could be based on fundamental principles of advanced consensus, such as fairness. In general a solution regarded as being "fair" lies in an equal split-up of the joint profit, i.e. the centre of the ZOPA. One problem of this equal split-up of the joint profit is that the ZOPA is often only known to the respective division. The divisions will not uncover their alternatives during negotiation, as it would be to their disadvantage during the course of negotiation.

NASH negotiation solution The NASH negotiation solution determines a transfer price that maximises the product of the profit increases (against the respective alternative) in both divisions within the according limits. This solution is the only one that fulfils the following five axiomatic requirements of a negotiation solution:

- Individual rationality (both divisions expect a positive profit).
- Symmetry (if the situations of both divisions are symmetrical).
- Pareto optimality.
- Independence against linear transformations.
- Independence against irrelevant alternatives.

Example: R is the transfer price to be found, and g_1 and g_2 are the respective opportunity costs of Division 1 and Division 2 if the internal transfer is not made. c_1 equals the variable costs of Division 1, and $cm_2 = p - c_2$ the preliminary contribution margin of Division 2 related to the same amount as in Division 1, then the transfer price is derived as follows:

$$\max_R [(R - c_1) - g_1] \cdot [(cm_2 - R) - g_2]$$

In the case of a zero-sum game (i.e. c_1 and cm_2 are constant) and if opportunity costs are $g_1 = g_2 = 0$, R lies right in the middle between c_1 and cm_2, i.e. $R = (c_1 + cm_2)/2$.

If transfer prices are negotiated, a **conciliation board** (for example, the management accountants) or a procedure to solve the conflicts is often inevitable. This can range from common agreements to assisting the search for a solution up to the determination of the transfer price by the conciliation board itself. It is important that the conciliation board is not addressed too often, as this would require a change in the procedure for the determination of the transfer prices.

5.2 A Hold up Model

At least in one way, negotiated transfer prices resemble transfer prices that contain a profit surcharge: they have the **disadvantage** of possibly holding up favourable investments of a division as the investing division carries the whole costs but only partially participates from the success of it. This so-called **hold up problem** is presented in the following simple example.

Assume that Division 1 produces an intermediate product, which is further processed by Division 2 and sold at the market. The **revenues** (sales) as a function of the production amount x equal:

$$S(x) = \alpha_2 - \beta \cdot x$$

The processing costs in Division 2 are $C_2(x) = c_2 \cdot x$. Division 1 can achieve a variable costs reduction in its division, for example, by innovation procedures, investments in cost cutting activities or employees' training. The production costs are $C_1(x, a)$, with a as **work productivity** or as an **investment**. The private costs of Division 1 amount to $v(a)$. Furthermore, the costs depend on an uncertain environmental condition θ. Simplifying, the following linear relationship is assumed:

$$C_1(x, a, \theta) = (c - a - \theta) \cdot x$$

In the first step, Division 1 must determine the level of its **work productivity**. This is done before the environmental condition θ is known. Once revealed, both divisions negotiate the transfer price and the amount to be transferred.

A determination of the transfer price after disclosure of θ enables a **risk-sharing** of the two divisions. With risk-averse divisional managers, this may lead to the acceptance of a risky order, due to the fact that part of the risk is transmitted to the supplying division via the transfer price depending on θ.

The **outcome of the negotiations** depends on the negotiating powers of both divisions. Assume that the divisions agree on the idea that the actual contribution margin from the sales of the products is shared "fairly" (but to not consider the advanced costs of the productivity level a). The contribution margin with productivity a and environmental condition θ follows as:

$$CM(x, \theta) = \underbrace{S(x) - C_2(x)}_{CM_2(x)} - C_1(x, a, \theta) = (\underbrace{\alpha_2 - c_2}_{\alpha} - \beta x) \cdot x - (c - a - \theta) \cdot x$$
$$= (\alpha - c + a + \theta - \beta x) \cdot x$$

It needs to be considered that the amount x is a function of a and θ as it is chosen after observation of these measures. To simplify, it is assumed that only direct functional dependences exist, for example, $CM = CM(x, \theta)$. Through the dependence of the amount x on a, CM also becomes dependent on a. The **split-up rule** should be that Division 1 receives a proportion γ of CM and Division 2 the remaining part $(1 - \gamma)$ with $\gamma \in [0, 1]$. A $\gamma = 0.5$ equals the Nash negotiation solution. The negotiated transfer price R^N arises from Division 1's proportion of the contribution margin and the production costs,

$$R^N(x,\theta) \cdot x = C_1(x,a,\theta) + \gamma \cdot CM(x,\theta)$$

Division 1 determines its amount by maximising its **profit**

$$R^N(x,\theta) \cdot x - C_1(x,a,\theta) + \gamma \cdot CM(x,\theta)$$

Division 2 maximises its profit

$$S(x) - C_2(x) - R^N(x,\theta) \cdot x = (1-\gamma) \cdot CM(x,\theta)$$

Both are interested in an ex post **efficient decision** about the amount $x(a, \theta)$, given a and θ. This arises from the maximisation of $CM(x, \theta)$ according to x,

$$\max_x CM(x,\theta) = (\alpha - c + a + \theta - \beta x) \cdot x$$

to

$$x^*(a,\theta) = \frac{\alpha - c + a + \theta}{2\beta}$$

Division 1 anticipates this decision and chooses its **productivity** a^N before observing θ by the maximisation of its expected profit

$$E\left[\gamma \cdot CM(x^*,\theta) - \frac{a^2}{2}\right] = E\left[\gamma \cdot \left(\frac{(\alpha - c + a + \theta)^2}{4\beta}\right) - \frac{a^2}{2}\right]$$

From this it is obvious that the chosen productivity level is not **optimal** from the head office's perspective, as long as $\gamma < 1$. Division 1 only receives a part γ of the gained advantage of its productivity, while it carries all of the costs, resulting in an **under investment** in productivity a compared to the situation in which the head office could decide the productivity level. Finally, the maximisation of Division 1's objective function proves an optimal productivity a^N of

$$a^N = \frac{\alpha - c + S[\theta]}{\frac{2\beta}{\gamma} - 1}$$

The productivity a^N rises in γ and reaches its maximum at $\gamma = 1$.

Monopoly Price-Based Transfer Price

Another variation to solve the **coordination problem** lies in the assignment of all the **negotiation power** for the transfer price to Division 1. Then, Division 1 determines the price after knowledge of θ (as a function of the demand), and Division 2 determines its resulting optimal amount. There is no negotiation anymore, and the head office devolves the negotiating authority to the divisions.

This approach equals a **monopolisation** of the supplying division. This is not identical to complete negotiation power ($\gamma = 1$), as Division 2 reacts to a given transfer price, while in the above described situation the amount and price were simultaneously determined. Division 1 utilises its knowledge of the **reaction function** of Division 2 to maximise its profit (the so-called **STACKELBERG solution**). Division 2 decides by the maximisation of its profit with a given transfer price $R(\theta)$

$$\begin{aligned}\max_x CM_2(x,\theta) &= S(x) - C_2(x) - R(\theta)x \\ &= (\alpha - R(\theta) - \beta x) \cdot x\end{aligned}$$

An optimal amount x^M arises from it:

$$x^M = \frac{\alpha - R(\theta)}{2\beta}$$

Now Division 1 determines the **transfer price** R^M by maximisation of its profit, with a given a and θ:

$$\max_R (R - c + a + \theta) \cdot \frac{\alpha - R}{2\beta}$$

From it arises as a transfer price

$$R^M = \frac{\alpha + c - a - \theta}{2}$$

R^M applied to the optimal amount x^M leads to x^M as half of the efficient amount x^*. This **production amount reduction** is an essential disadvantage of such a transfer price system. It results from the monopoly price determination.

The **inefficient decision** also induces ex ante an inefficient level of **productivity**. Before observation of θ Division 1 maximises the expected profit, taking into account the following decisions with regard to the transfer price and the induced amount. **The expected profit** amounts to

$$E\left[(R - c + a + \theta) \cdot \frac{\alpha - R}{2\beta} - \frac{a^2}{2}\right] = E\left[\left(\frac{(\alpha - c + a + \theta)^2}{8\beta}\right) - \frac{a^2}{2}\right]$$

By derivation toward a, the optimal productivity a^M arises as

$$a^M = \frac{\alpha - c + S[\theta]}{4\beta - 1}$$

A **comparison** of the productivity a^M with the level of activity arising with a negotiated transfer price a^N shows that

$$a^N = \frac{\alpha - c + S[\theta]}{\frac{2\beta}{\gamma} - 1} > a^M = \frac{\alpha - c + S[\theta]}{4\beta - 1} \Leftrightarrow \gamma > \frac{1}{2}$$

If the **ex post negotiation power** of Division 1 is higher than that of Division 2 ($\gamma > 0.5$), then Division 1 has the incentive to increase its productivity with this negotiated transfer price, compared to a monopoly price-based transfer price. Since the ex post amounts at the same time are **efficient**, this implies that negotiated transfer prices with $\gamma \geq 0.5$ are superior, in a short-term perspective of the head office, than the monopoly price-based variation. However, for $\gamma < 0.5$ this result can be reversed: the ex post inefficient **amount decisions** can be counterbalanced by higher incentives to increase **productivity**.

Chapter 6
Transfer Prices and Behavioural Control

Abstract Transfer prices generate an internal market, and are applied for behavioural control. They are therefore also used for cost management and strategy penetration, for the coordination of price decisions and as a strategic means. A case study summarizes the different types and shows a Nash solution by which it can be illustrated that the real optimum typically cannot be achieved by decentralised decision-making.

Keywords Cost management · Strategy penetration · Product development · Coordination · Nash equilibrium · Distributive effect · Productive effect · Optimal prices · Centralised organisation · Decentralised organisation · Strategic transfer prices

The focus of the analysis so far has been the coordination of internally transferred amounts between the production and purchasing divisions with a sequential production. However, coordination can encompass another level: in the following, examples of cost management and strategy penetration are discussed to examine the issue of transfer prices from a slightly different perspective.

6.1 Introduction

Transfer prices and cost allocations can serve as an instrument of (personnel) coordination if a decentralised decision-maker (e.g. manager, employee) pursues other objectives than the head office and when the head office has no sufficient means to directly affect the decisions. With the help of a cost allocation chosen in a meaningful way, the decision problem is distorted in such a way that the decision-maker himself chooses a decision that meets the objective of the company as a whole.

P. Schuster, *Transfer Prices and Management Accounting*,
SpringerBriefs in Accounting, DOI 10.1007/978-3-319-14750-5_6

Behavioural control is basically achieved by **influencing** the **price structure of the input factors**. Prerequisites for efficiency are:

- The manager applies the price of the internal product for his decision-making.
- The decision is **sensitive** to the price of the internal product.
- The decision influences the **objective measure** used for assessing the decision-maker's performance.
- The transfer price is found acceptable by the decision-maker.

In many cases, deliberately **distorted** costs appear, i.e. they are allocated too high or too low. The divisional manager is supposed to optimise the distorted divisional profit, and at the same time the performance measurement and manager assessment must be made based on this distorted divisional profit, even if is known that this is not the "correct" profit. This typically contradicts the **profit allocation function** of transfer prices.

6.2 Cost Management and Strategy Penetration

Transfer prices generate an internal market. Depending on the extent by which the divisions may use an external market, different internal market forms arise. If supply and purchase limits exist, a bilateral **monopoly** results. Both divisions typically act sensitively to price changes, and a higher price will reduce the demand for the internal product and with it, the amount transferred internally, even if the producing division wanted to offer higher quantities. A lower price will reduce the supply and with it the transferred amount. Similar relations apply for other "market" configurations. The head office can use this "market" to induce certain **behaviours** of divisional managers. Some examples are discussed in the following paragraph.

Products or production procedures can be presented as less expensive to guide the product manager's behaviour. Short-term profit maximisation can be affected by a "subsidy" of long-term decisions. On account of his short **planning horizon**, assume that a divisional manager invests too little in research and development. From the perspective of the head office, they can influence this by offering results of a central research department for a transfer price below its costs.

Another *example*: the head office has the impression that the management accounting department produces too many reports beyond the informational need of the users. The demand can be limited by determination of specific (transfer) prices, and a division will then only "buy" a report, when its utility exceeds these costs.

Another *example*: a company produces video recorders in several divisions. The head office is convinced that competitive advantages can only be gained by speeding up **automation**. The central overhead costs are allocated on the basis of direct labour to the separate divisions. This leads to an indirect **rise** of overhead allocated on the basis of direct labour costs and to a relative preference for automated production processes in the view of the divisions. It is interesting to note that cost allocation obviously is against the causation of the costs, but this is irrelevant, as only the induced effect is important.

Additionally, it is interesting to note that the pressure for automation will be stronger for a division when other divisions are already heavily automated. This exemplifies possible advantages of cost allocations against transfer prices. **Cost allocations** are transfer prices that fulfil an additional condition: that the sum of the allocated costs equals the costs incurred. Thus, if a higher amount is allocated to one division, another division will face lower amounts allocated.

Behavioural control in product development

A product developer or technical designer often attributes essentially greater value to the technical elegance of a product solution than does the market and company management. However, due to the lack of expert knowledge, he cannot decide about the sufficient development time that actually is necessary. Therefore, upper management cannot prescribe this development time, but does possess some indirect possibilities to guide the product developer to greater efficiency from the company's perspective.

For example, the "imputed" overhead costs can be charged on a basis exceeding the true costs, with the effect that the costs of development hours raises. To avoid endangering the introduction of a new product on account of high costs, the product developer will be careful to spend less time on inefficient design or engage in excessive trialling of different designs. Similar effects can be raised by charging distorted costs for needed parts: standard parts can be charged too low, and special parts relatively too high, to motivate the product developer to prefer the use of standard parts.

6.3 Coordination of Price Decisions

The following case study analyses the coordination of divisions with existing market interdependencies. **Competitive situations** between divisions can happen in decentralised organisation, just as also with external competitors.

Case Study Assumptions

Division 1 produces the electronic control unit, S1, that is used for the final products. Division 2 specialises in analogous technology, and Division 3 in digital technology. Among other products both divisions produce the measuring instruments, M2 and M3, both of which need the electronic control unit of Division 1. The organisational form has been chosen as the technology applied is one of the essential specialisation aspects that requires the division of activities.

The variable costs of S1 amount to 10, the subsequent processing costs for the production of M2 an additional 10 and of M3 an additional 15. There are no effective capacity limits. To a certain extent, both instruments, M2 and M3, are substitutes in the market. The following price demand functions describe the market (x_i equals the amount of the instrument M_i and p_i its price for $i = 2, 3$):

$$\text{Instrument M2: } x_2 = 100 - 2p_2 + p_3$$
$$\text{Instrument M3: } x_3 = 200 - 2p_3 + p_2$$

Both managers determine their optimal price from their respective perspective based on a **Nash equilibrium**. The optimal price of M2 arises from the maximisation of the contribution margin CM_2:

$$\max_{p_2} CM_2 = (p_2 - c_2) \cdot x_2 = (p_2 - c_2) \cdot (100 - 2p_2 + p_3)$$

and $c_2 = 10 + R$. The first derivation is

$$\frac{\partial CM_2}{\partial p_2} = 100 - 2p_2 + p_3 - 2p_2 + 2c_2$$

Setting this equation to zero leads to the **optimal price** as a function of the price of M3,

$$p_2^* = \frac{1}{4} \cdot (100 + 2c_2 + p_3)$$

Analogously, the optimal price of M3 arises by maximisation of CM_3 to:

$$p_3^* = \frac{1}{4} \cdot (200 + 2c_3 + p_2)$$

The mutually rational expectations about the price determination result in optimal prices at the Nash equilibrium. If these optimal prices are applied in the reaction function of the respective division, the following **optimal prices and amounts** arise as:

$$p_2^* = \frac{1}{15} \cdot (600 + 8c_2 + 2c_3), \quad p_3^* = \frac{1}{15} \cdot (900 + 8c_3 + 2c_2)$$
$$x_2^* = \frac{2}{15} \cdot (600 - 7c_2 + 2c_3), \quad x_3^* = \frac{2}{15} \cdot (900 - 7c_3 + 2c_2)$$

None of the divisions can improve its profit by a unilateral change of its price, given the optimal price of the other division. The **transfer price** R for the control unit S1 is found in the variable costs of both divisions, i.e. $c_2 = 10 + R$ and $c_3 = 15 + R$. In the following section, the effects of several transfer price types on the achieved contribution margins are analysed.

Transfer Price Equalling the Variable Costs

The results are summarised in Table 6.1. Division 1 achieves a contribution margin of zero by the internal trade. Division 3 can use the favourable market conditions despite higher costs of M3 and achieves a contribution margin of more than twice the amount of the contribution margin of Division 2.

Table 6.1 Initial solution

	Division 1	Division 2	Division 3
Unit cost	10	20	25
Transfer price or optimal price	10	54	76
Sales volume	170	68	102
Divisional contribution margin	0	2,312	5,202
Total contribution margin			7,514

Table 6.2 Solution with market price

	Division 1	Division 2	Division 3
Unit cost	10	35	40
Transfer price or optimal price	25	64	86
Sales volume	150	58	92
Divisional contribution margin	2,250	1,682	4,232
Total contribution margin			8,164

Transfer Price Equalling the Market Price

Assume that the market price for S1 is 25. In this case, unit costs for both purchasing divisions are 15 higher, and both divisions analogously determine their new optimal prices, which now lie appropriately higher. The consequence is that Division 1 achieves a positive contribution margin and the contribution margins of the two other divisions are cut. Table 6.2 states the results of this situation.

The essential result of this situation is the fact that the total contribution margin has risen by almost 9 %. Clearly, two effects of the transfer price can be recognised:

1. **Distributive effect**: the transfer price redistributes the total contribution margin between the supplying and purchasing division.
2. **Productive effect**: the total contribution margin is changed. This is a consequence of the behavioural control.

The transfer price changes the **relevant unit costs** for managers of Divisions 2 and 3 and with it, their price behaviour. They set higher prices for their instruments. This decreases the expected sales and, as can be expected, has negative consequences for both divisional contribution margins. However, the loss is lower than the gain achieved by the supplying Division 1. The reason for this is the substitutive relationship of the two instruments M2 and M3. A coordination of the prices typically leads to higher prices, than in the case where the divisions act like independent companies in competition. However, the decentralised profit centre organisation does not enable such coordination, because both divisions must only regard their own profits. Finally, they are also assessed by them.

Table 6.3 Solution with the optimal transfer price

	Division 1	Division 2	Division 3
Unit cost	10.00	51.88	56.88
Transfer price or optimal price	41.88	75.25	97.25
Sales volume	127.50	46.75	80.75
Divisional contribution margin	4,064.06	1,092.78	3,260.28
Total contribution margin			8,417.13

Optimal Transfer Price

The optimal transfer price from the perspective of the head office (the company as a whole) maximises the **sum of the contribution margins** of all three divisions from the autonomous decentralised price policy for both Divisions 2 and 3, i.e.

$$\max_{8} \underbrace{(R-10)\cdot(x_2^*+x_3^*)}_{CM_1} + \underbrace{(p_2^*-10-R)\cdot x_2^*}_{CM_2} + \underbrace{(p_3^*-15-R)\cdot x_3^*}_{CM_3}$$

Finally, if the appropriate equations for the prices and amounts that depend on R are used, an optimal transfer price of $R = 41.875$ arises. Table 6.3 presents the results. Division 1 gains the highest contribution margin of all involved divisions with this transfer price. Attention should be paid to the fact that the purchasing Divisions 2 and 3 must be forced to buy internally from Division 1, as the market price of 25 (if necessary, plus procurement side costs) lies essentially below this transfer price. Therefore, the head office must limit the Divisions' autonomy.

Fundamentally, the use of the **market price** as a transfer price does not solve the coordination problem. This is completely independent from the known problems with the determination of "the" market price. The **optimal transfer price** also has no relation to the relevant costs of the intermediate product. It also does not depend on whether a division achieves a profit or not. Up to now, capacity costs (fixed costs) were not introduced at all; and they are not required for the result. The optimal transfer price is dependent on the market situation and also on the cost situation in the purchasing division.

If the final products were complementary instead of substitutive, the prices would have to be set lower for M2 and M3 than in the initial solution (Table 6.1). The transfer price would then be below variable costs, and Division 1 would always achieve a negative contribution margin.

This example clearly shows the **conflict** between the **coordination function** and the **profit allocation function** of the transfer price. The divisional contribution margin does not adequately measure the performance of the respective divisions. Certainly, Division 1 is not the sole division contributing to the company's success. Due to the profit linkage on account of the market interdependence, the individual division's success and performance cannot be precisely separated.

Centralised Organisation
For a comparison of decentralised organisation versus centralised organisation, it is now assumed that the head office possesses full information about the situations in both divisions and determines the sales prices of both instruments itself. Then the head office maximises:

$$\begin{aligned}\max_{P_2,P_3}(CM_1 + CM_2 + CM_3) &= 0 + (p_2 - c_2) \cdot x_2 + (p_3 - c_3) \cdot x_3 \\ &= (p_2 - 20) \cdot (100 - 2p_2 + p_3) \\ &\quad + (p_3 - 25) \cdot (200 - 2p_3 + p_2)\end{aligned}$$

This leads to optimal prices $p_2^* = 76.67$ and $p_3^* = 95.83$ as well to a **total profit** of 8,429.17. This solution would only be attainable with a transfer price system, if the transfer prices of both divisions could be set at different amounts (in this case, for Division 2 a little bit higher and for Division 3 a little bit lower than 41.875).

6.4 Strategic Transfer Prices

Another important function of internal transfer prices is their **relational effect** in regard to external competition. If a market equilibrium with simultaneous decision-making about prices (price competition in a BERTRAND equilibrium) or production/sales volumes (COURNOT equilibrium) is assumed, a company can gain **competitive advantages** against its **competitors**, when it is able to commit itself to certain decisions in advance. Thereupon, the (rational) competitor must make its own decision as to the best response to the strategy of the company. Typically, this situation evolves into a disadvantage for the competitor company.

The basic idea is illustrated by a **specific situation** (adapted from Göx 1999). Assume that two companies are in price competition and their (inverse) price demand functions are symmetrical and given as

$$x_1 = \alpha - p_1 + \beta \cdot p_i \tag{6.4.1}$$

for $i, j = 1, 2$ and $i \neq j$. The variable production costs per unit are identical for both companies $c > 0$, and no fixed costs occur. It further applies $a > c$ and $0 < b < 1$. The price demand function describes (partial) substitute products.

If no company can engage itself in a specific price strategy, the market equilibrium is achieved by the following situation. Every company determines its reaction function, i.e. the strategic response to the competitor, by maximisation of its profit function:

$$\begin{aligned}\pi_1 &= (p_i - c) \cdot x_i = (p_i - c) \cdot (\alpha - p_i + \beta \cdot p_i) \\ \frac{\partial \pi_1}{\partial p_1} &= \alpha - 2p_i + \beta p_j + c = 0\end{aligned} \tag{6.4.2}$$

As both companies face the same situation, this condition is also considered for p_j. By applying p_j into p_i, it finally results in the **equilibrium prices**

$$p_i^* = \frac{\alpha + c}{2 - \beta} \quad \text{for } i = 1, 2. \tag{6.4.3}$$

Finally, **the profit** of each company amounts to:

$$\pi_i^* = \frac{(\alpha - (1 - \beta) \cdot c)^2}{(2 - \beta)^2} \tag{6.4.4}$$

Now it is assumed that each company **decentralises** its **price decision** by hiring a **manager** and asking him to maximise the divisional profit of his profit centre. Similar effects arise, if only one enterprise decentralises its decision-making. At the same time, the respective head office sets the transfer price R for the input factors. This is generally known. The **divisional profit** is:

$$\pi_i^D = (p_i - R) \cdot (\alpha - p_i + \beta \cdot p_j) \tag{6.4.5}$$

With an analogous calculation to (6.4.3), both managers determine their **sales prices** as follows:

$$p_i^D = \frac{\alpha + R}{2 - \beta} \quad \text{for } i = 1, 2. \tag{6.4.6}$$

However, the **profit of the companies** is determined on the basis of the real costs c and not the transfer price R. With the given transfer price, it is:

$$\pi_i^{strategic} = (p_i^D - c) \cdot x_i = \left(\frac{\alpha + R}{2 - \beta} - c \right) \cdot \frac{\alpha - (1 - \beta)R}{2 - \beta} \tag{6.4.7}$$

According to the transfer price R, the optimisation of (6.4.7) supplies the following condition, and both companies again choose the same transfer price as a result of the symmetry of the situation:

$$\frac{\partial \pi_i^{strategic}}{\partial R} = \frac{1}{(2 - \beta)^2} \cdot [\alpha - (1 - \beta) \cdot R - (1 - \beta) \cdot (\alpha + R - 2c + \beta \cdot c)] = 0$$

Finally, the **optimal transfer price** arises as:

$$R_i^* = \frac{\alpha \cdot \beta + c \cdot (2 - \beta) \cdot (1 - \beta)}{2 \cdot (1 - \beta)} = c + \frac{\beta \cdot (\alpha - (1 - \beta) \cdot c)}{2 \cdot (1 - \beta)} > c \tag{6.4.8}$$

The optimal transfer price is higher than the variable costs per unit (because $\alpha > c$ the fraction is higher than zero). In other words: the transfer price has a strategic effect. If (6.4.8) is set into (6.4.7), the profit is:

$$\pi_i^{strategic} = \frac{(\alpha - (1 - \beta) \cdot c)^2}{4 - 4\beta} \tag{6.4.9}$$

A comparison of (6.4.9) with (6.4.4) shows that $\pi_i^{strategic}$ is higher for all $\beta > 0$ than π_i^* and that the difference rises with β.

The **reason** for this effect of the transfer price is that the price, which the managers require in the equilibrium, rises with the transfer price. A higher price of both companies reduces the strength of the competition in the market, and finally both companies profit from it. The stronger the competition, i.e. the higher b, the more distinctive is the advantage of the strategic transfer price. This is a comparable effect to the one shown in the last section, with two divisions of the same company competing at the market.

Why is this solution only possible with decentralised price decision-making and introduction of a transfer price? Without decentralisation, the announcement by one of the companies of a price higher than the equilibrium price would not be credible or trustworthy. For example, if one company would choose a higher price p_i instead of its equilibrium price p_i^*, the other company could improve its position on account of its optimal reaction function (6.4.2) by choice of a new price $p_j(p_i)$. The definition of the market equilibrium shows that there is only one pair of prices (p_i^*, p_j^*), from which no company wants to individually deviate. However, the contract with the manager by which he is urged to maximise his divisional profit under the given transfer price gives **credibility** to a higher price, as the manager sets this price in his own best interest. From the perspective of the company, the manager is used only to set a price strategy divergent from the original equilibrium, in a convincing way. However, a prerequisite is that the contracts and the transfer prices are observable and cannot be later amended.

Chapter 7
Summary

The **main functions** of transfer prices are **coordination** of management and **profit allocation** of decentralised units. They are an instrument of the **company organisation** and must be regarded and evaluated in conjunction with other instruments, for example, sales and purchase limits.

Transfer prices are necessary to be able to determine separate **divisional profits** despite **interdependencies** between the divisions, particularly mutual product transfers; and are necessary too, to use them to assess the profitability of the divisions and the activities of divisional management. **Market-based transfer prices** are suitable when there is a (nearly) perfect market for the internal products, if only low synergistic effects exist or the transfer volume is relatively small. The divisions then act as if they were independent companies.

In the reality of company practice, **cost-based transfer prices** are the most frequently used types. Transfer prices based on **marginal costs** fulfil the coordination function for short-term decisions under certain circumstances; however, for the assessment of divisions, they are not suitable, because they typically discriminate the producing division. Transfer prices based on **full costs** can represent a good **approximation** for the relevant costs in long-term perspective. However, they typically lead to incorrect decisions in the short-term view, particularly if they contain a profit surcharge. A special form of transfer prices on a full cost basis, is a **two-tier transfer price**. Each transaction is based on marginal costs, and for the capacity supplied, a certain fixed amount per period is determined. **Full costs plus a profit surcharge**, as a transfer price, can have negative effects on several decisions but can also be favourable if the productivity of a division is unknown.

Dual transfer prices equal different transfer prices for the producing and buying divisions. They are hardly regarded as being acceptable in practice, as the sum of the divisional profits exceeds the total profit of the company.

With asymmetrically distributed information, all cost-based transfer prices potentially lead to **incentives** for distorted and untruthful cost reporting and can cause incorrect decisions from the perspective of the company as a whole.

P. Schuster, *Transfer Prices and Management Accounting*,
SpringerBriefs in Accounting, DOI 10.1007/978-3-319-14750-5_7

Negotiated transfer prices exemplify and bestow the greatest possible autonomy of divisional managers with potentially positive motivational effects. If the divisions possess a high level of knowledge of the mutual situations, better decisions can arise, than when the head office prescribes a transfer price. However, negotiations can lead to conflicts within the company. Transfer prices can be applied to **risk sharing**, if they are not chosen as being constant, but depend on environmental situations.

The coordination function of transfer prices and cost allocations can be used for **behavioural control** of divisional managers, if the transfer prices are strategically set.

Decentralised organisation, e.g. a profit centre-organisation, is installed for improving entrepreneurial conducts of managers. Yet, there is no such thing as an ideal solution for transfer prices and there‘s not even a "fair" transfer price.

The conflict between coordination and profit allocation, i.e. decentralised decisions that are in the best interest of the company as a whole on the one hand, and transfer prices that allow the calculation of reliable and trustworthy divisional profits on the other hand, is evident in most of the examples shown in this book. The divisional contribution margins and profits, as illustrated in the case study, do not adequately measure the performance of the respective division. Decentralised decision-making, applying any type of the transfer prices discussed, did not find the real optimum solution.

Transfer prices, as seen, are of dominant importance in the reality of company practice and deserve high focus and increased attention in the area of Management Accounting.

Chapter 8
Assessment Material

8.1 Review Questions

1. To what extent does a conflict exist between the different functions of transfer prices?
2. Under which circumstances does coordination by the market not lead to the total optimum?
3. What causes the difference between a market-based transfer price with or without sales and purchase limits for the intermediate product at the external market?
4. Can the use of the market price as a transfer price lead to arbitrary profit allocations of the affected divisions?
5. When do marginal cost-based transfer prices lead to optimal coordination?
6. Does the supplying division with a marginal cost-based transfer price always incur a loss, and if so, how could the transfer price be modified to exclude this?
7. What is the reason that causes a dual transfer price system to achieve optimal coordination? Can it be profitable for a division to distort its information, and if so, in which direction?
8. Transfer prices, which are negotiated by the divisions involved, potentially cause conflicts. A company determines the following conciliation procedure: if the divisions do not agree within an appropriate time, the transfer price is prescribed by the group controller with full costs plus a 3 % profit surcharge. What effect does this have on the negotiation of the divisions?
9. Can the head office force the divisions to always report truthfully? If so, is this more favourable or unfavourable for the head office than a situation in which the divisions can supply distorted information—with the head office considering this?
10. Many companies impose a so-called last call principle, according to which the supplying division can receive the same conditions as an external customer of the buying division. What advantages and disadvantages does such a principle have?

P. Schuster, *Transfer Prices and Management Accounting*,
SpringerBriefs in Accounting, DOI 10.1007/978-3-319-14750-5_8

11. What types of transfer prices can be derived in an agency model?
12. What advantages and disadvantages does a cost allocation based on the average principle, have?
13. How can the allocation of fixed costs be economically justified for divisions that do not make the decision that causes these fixed costs themselves?
14. What advantages could divisions identify for arranging a given cost split-up plan?
15. Under which conditions, and why, can it be profitable to employ a manager and to impose on him a transfer price above the costs for the internal transfers?

8.2 Exercise 1: HIRSHLEIFER Model

A company is divided into three divisions: Division 1 produces an intermediate product and supplies it to Division 2. Division 2 processes this and sells it as an intermediate product to Division 3, which converts it into a marketable final product. There is no market for the two intermediate products.

(a) Determine the optimum transfer prices so that all divisions choose the same amounts that lead to maximising the company's profit. The corporate head office has insight into the following divisions' cost functions and the price demand curve:

 Division 1: $C_1(x) = 20 + \frac{x^3}{6}$
 Division 2: $C_2(x) = 60 + \frac{x^2}{2}$
 Division 3: $C_3(x) = 45 + x^3$
 Price demand curve: $p(x) = 108 - \frac{x^2}{6}$

(b) Division 2 anticipates its loss situation and decides to inform the head office of a modified cost function. Calculate the effects on the company's profit and for the reported profits of the individual divisions if Division 2 announces the function as $\hat{C}_2(x) = 60 + x^2$.
(c) If Division 2 announces that the modified cost function is

$$\hat{C}_2(x) = 100 + \frac{x^2}{2},$$

what effect does it have on the overall profit results?

8.3 Exercise 2: Dual Transfer Prices

Division 1 produces an intermediate product costing

$$C_1(x) = 40 + \frac{x^3}{6}$$

and supplies it to Division 2, where it is further processed into a marketable product at costs of:

$$C_2(x) = 35 + x^2.$$

There is no market for the intermediate product. The price demand function is $p(x) = 82.295 - 0.05x$.

Determine the dual transfer prices at which the head office can motivate the profit-optimising amount in the interest of the company as a whole. How high are divisional profits if you use dual transfer prices?

8.4 Exercise 3: Cost Allocations

The IT department is organised as a central service of a company. The costs of providing the central services amount to 1,200. To simplify matters, let us assume that we are only dealing with fixed costs (such as labour costs and depreciation). Plans indicate that two divisions draw on different IT services as follows:

Planned requirement	D1	D2	Capacity
PC and software maintenance	15	9	30
Internet access	15	3	30
Central ordering	6	5	12

If each division were to install its own IT or buy in the service from outside, this would result in costs for Division 1 of about 1,000 and for Division 2 of about 500. The divisions' results before allocating the IT costs are 2,000 for Division 1 and 1,600 for Division 2. How high are the divisional results after the allocation of the IT costs?

8.5 Exercise 4: Cost Allocations

For the produced level of x, a production process causes costs of: $C(x) = \sqrt{x}$. The company consists of one division producing (indexed at 0) and three divisions, B_1, B_2 and B_3, buying in. They buy in the amounts $x_1 = 3$, $x_2 = 5$ and $x_3 = 2$. The total costs (rounded) are:

$$C_0(x) = \sqrt{10} = 3.162$$

(a) How high is the cost advantage from performing centralised production?
(b) What is the minimum and maximum amount that should be allocated to each division?
(c) How should the costs $C_0 = 3.162$ be divided between the three divisions?

8.6 Exercise 5: Full Cost Allocation (Adapted from Magee 1986, p. 338 f)

Borel manufactures all kinds of toys driven by a small electric motor. Division A produces the electric motors. Division B specialises in little railways manufactured using injection-moulding technology, installs the motors and eventually sells them. Division B's variable costs are more or less constant for the railways at an average of 100. The fixed costs are 34,000 per month. The company currently produces around 4,000 railways per month sold at an average price of 200. Division A generally passes on the costs of the electric motors monthly to the divisions asking for them. The (monthly) cost function is

$$C(x) = 100,000 + 50x$$

Besides division B, division C also needs electric motors. Its requirements, however, are extremely volatile with the most recent estimates indicating a need for 2,000 or 6,000 motors with an equal level of probability in each case.

Now division B receives an additional order of 2,000 railways at a special price of 154.50 each.

(a) Assume that division B wants to maximise its divisional profit. Should it accept the additional order or not?
(b) B's divisional manager receives a bonus for a monthly profit in excess of 100,000. Will this affect his decision on the additional order?

8.7 Exercise 6: Cost Allocations and Capacity Adjustments (Adapted from Magee 1986, p. 341 f)

OX Ltd has seen strong growth in recent years. Management has now suggested considering hiring a commercial lawyer who could do the advisory work in-house which had previously been given to two law practices. The management accountant, Thomas Prad, who is involved in this, has the following data. The law practices charge 200 per hour on average. The commercial lawyer with a secretary would probably cost 200,000 p.a. The problem is that the number of hours of advisory work needed each year is uncertain. Thomas Prad had the impression from discussions that OX Ltd's two divisions knew very well how many hours of advisory work they needed, but did not want to be pinned down by him. The two divisional managers are each interested in maximising their respective divisional profits. Based on his own research, Thomas derives the following probabilities of hours needed:

	400 h	500 h	600 h
Division 1	50 %	50 %	–
Division 2	–	50 %	50 %

The controller, Thomas Prad, now faces the task of determining the pros and cons of setting up a legal department.

(a) Based on Thomas's ex ante level of information, should the department be set up or not?
(b) Assume that Thomas would like to motivate the two divisions to declare their actual needs. To this end, he proposes to the two divisional managers that the in-house advisory work will be made available free of charge. What will the divisional managers claim and what will be the decision on the department?
(c) What would happen if Thomas proposes that the divisions be allocated the 200,000 in costs based on the figures given by them for their requirements?
(d) What would happen if the proposal looked like this: each division declares its requirements for hours of advisory work and the legal department will only be set up if the total is equal to or greater than 1,000, whereby 40 % of the costs will be allocated to Division 1 and 60 % to Division 2?

References

Anthony, R. N., Dearden, J., & Govindarajan, V. (1992). *Management control systems* (7th ed.). Boston, MA: Irwin.

Aryva, A., & Mittendorf, B. (2007). Interacting supply chain distortions: The pricing of internal transfers and external procurement. *The Accounting Review, 82*(3), 551–580.

Aryva, A., & Mittendorf, B. (2011). Supply chains and segment profitability: How input pricing creates a latent cross-segment subsidy. *The Accounting Review, 86*(3), 805–824.

Balachandran, B. V., Li, L., & Magee, R. P. (1987). On the allocation of fixed and variable costs from service departments. *Contemporary Accounting Research, 4*(1), 164–185 (Autumn).

Baldenius, T., Melumad, N. D., & Reichelstein, S. (2004). Integrating managerial and tax objectives in transfer pricing. *The Accounting Review, 79*(3), 591–615.

Baldenius, T., & Reichelstein, S. (2006). External and internal pricing in multidivisional firms. *Journal of Accounting Research, 44*(1), 1–28.

Borkowski, S. C. (1988). *An investigation into the divergence of theory from practice regarding transfer pricing methods*. Ph.D. Thesis, Temple University.

Borkowski, S. C. (1990). Environmental and organizational factors affecting transfer pricing: A survey. *Management Accounting Research, 1*(2), 78–99.

Cook, P. (1955). Decentralization and the transfer-price problem. *The Journal of Business, 28*(2) January, 87–94.

Deloitte. (2006). *Teile eines Ganzen—Empirische Studie zur Steuerung von Konzernen mit transnationaler Wertschöpfung*.www.deloitte.de.

Dean, J. (1955, July–August). Decentralization and intracompany pricing. *Harvard Business Review, 33*(4), 65–74.

Eccles, R. G. (1985). *The transfer pricing problem*. Lexington, MA: Lexington Books.

Ernst & Young. (2003). *Transfer pricing 2003 global survey*. www.ey.com.

Ewert, R., & Wagenhofer, A. (2014). *Interne Unternehmensrech-nung* (8th ed.). Berlin: Springer.

Gjerdrum, J., Shah, N., & Papageorgiou, L. G. (2002). Fair transfer price and inventory holding policies in two-enterprise supply chains. *European Journal of Operational Research, 143*(3), 582–599.

Göx, R. F. (1999). *Strategische Transferpreispolitik*. Wiesbaden.

Göx, R. F., & Shiller, U. (2007). An economic perspective on transfer pricing. In C. S. Chapmann, A. G. Hopwood, & M. D. Shields (Eds.), *Handbook of management accounting research* (Vol. 2, pp. 673–695). Amsterdam: Elsevier.

Grabski, S. V. (1985). Transfer pricing in complex organizations: A review and integration of recent empirical and analytical research. *Journal of Accounting Literature, 4*, 33–75.

Hirshleifer, J. (1956). On the economics of transfer pricing. *Journal of Business, 29*, 172–184.

P. Schuster, *Transfer Prices and Management Accounting*,
SpringerBriefs in Accounting, DOI 10.1007/978-3-319-14750-5

Hirshleifer, J. (1957). Economics of the decentralized firm. *Journal of Business, 30*, 96–108.

Ijiri, Y. (1967). *The foundations of accounting measurement: A mathematical, economic, and behavioral inquiry*. Englewood Cliffs, NJ: Prentice-Hall.

Kachelmeier, S. J., & Towry, K. L. (2002, July). Negotiated transfer pricing: Is fairness easier said than done? *The Accounting Review, 77*(3), 571–593.

Kaplan, R. S., & Atkinson, A. A. (1998). *Advanced management accounting* (3rd ed.). Englewood Cliffs, NJ: Prentice-Hall.

Lakhal, S. Y. (2006). An operational profit sharing and transfer pricing model for network-manufacturing companies. *European Journal of Operational Research, 175*(1), 543–565.

Lakhal, S. Y., H'Mida, S., & Venkatadri, U. (2005). A market-driven transfer price for distributed products using mathematical programming. *European Journal of Operational Research, 162*(3), 690–699.

Lambert, D. R. (1979). Transfer pricing and interdivisional conflicts. *California Management Review, 21*, 70–75.

Lantz, B. (2009). The double marginalization problem of transfer pricing: Theory and experiment. *European Journal of Operational Research, 196*(2), 434–439.

Li, S.-H., & Balachandran, K. R. (1997). Optimal transfer pricing schemes for work averse division managers with private information. *European Journal of Operational Research, 98*(1), 138–153.

Magee, R. P. (1986). *Advanced management accounting*. New York: Harper and Row.

McAulay, L., & Tomkins, C. R. (1992). A review of the contemporary transfer pricing literature with recommendations for future research. *British Journal of Management, 3*, 101–122.

McAulay, L., Scrace, A., & Tomkins, C. R. (2001). Transferring priorities: A three-act play on transfer pricing. *Critical Perspectives on Accounting, 12*, 87–113.

Miller, B. L., & Buckman, A. G. (1987). Cost allocation and opportunity costs. *Management Science, 33*(5), 626–638.

Pfaff, D., & Stefani, U. (2006). Verrechnungspreise in der Unternehmenspraxis. *Controlling* (pp. 517–524).

Pfeiffer, T. (1999). Transfer pricing and decentralized dynamic lot-sizing in multistage, multiproduct production processes. *European Journal of Operational Research, 116*(2), 319–330.

Ronen, J., & McKinney, G. (1970). Transfer pricing for divisional autonomy. *Journal of Accounting, 8*, 99–112.

Samuels, J. (1969). Penalties and subsidies in internal pricing policies. *Journal of Business Finance, 1*(3), 31–38.

Sappington, D. (1983). Limited liability contracts between principal and agent. *Journal of Economic Theory, 29*, 1–21.

Schuster, P., & Clarke, P. (2010). Transfer prices: Functions, types, and behavioral implications. *Management Accounting Quarterly, 11*(2), 22–32.

Seed, A. H. (1970). The rational abuse of accounting information. *Management Accounting*, January, 9–11.

Thomas, A. L. (1980). *A behavioural analysis of joint-cost allocation and transfer pricing*. Champaign: Stipes Publishing Company.

Tomkins, C. (1990). Making sense of cost-plus transfer prices where there are imperfect intermediate good markets by a 'pragmatic-analytical' perspective. *Management Accounting Research, 1*(3), 199–216.

Vancil, R. F. (1979). *Decentralization—managerial ambiguity by design*. New York: Financial Executives Research Foundation.

Vidal, C. J., & Goetschalckx, M. (2001). A global supply chain model with transfer pricing and transportation cost allocation. *European Journal of Operational Research, 129*(1), 134–158.

Villegas, F., & Ouenniche, J. (2008). A general unconstrained model for transfer pricing in multinational supply chains. *European Journal of Operational Research, 187*(3), 829–856.

Wagenhofer, A. (1992). Verrechnungspreise zur Koordination bei Informationsasymmetrie. In K. Spreman, & E. Zur (Eds.). *Controlling* (pp. 637–656). Wiesbaden: Gabler Verlag

Wagenhofer, A. (1994). Transfer pricing under asymmetric information. *European Accounting Review*, *3*, 71–104.
Watson, J. H., & Baumler, J. V. (1975). Transfer pricing: A behavioral context. *The Accounting Review*, *50*(3), 466–474.
Wu, F. H., & Sharp, D. (1979). An empirical study of transfer pricing practice. *International Journal of Accounting, Spring*, 71–79.
Zverovich, S., & Schuster, P. (2015). Transfer pricing in non-linear revenue settings. *The International Journal of Management Accounting Research, 4* (in print).

MIX
Papier aus verantwortungsvollen Quellen
Paper from responsible sources
FSC® C105338

If you have any concerns about our products,
you can contact us on
ProductSafety@springernature.com

In case Publisher is established outside the EU,
the EU authorized representative is:
Springer Nature Customer Service Center GmbH
Europaplatz 3, 69115 Heidelberg, Germany

Printed by Libri Plureos GmbH
in Hamburg, Germany